A Faculty Guide for Succeeding in Academe

All too often a culture of silence permeates academia, where faculty and administrators ignore or misunderstand difficult situations. *A Faculty Guide for Succeeding in Academe* is a practical guide for prospective and current faculty that addresses real, complex issues that are too often left unexamined. Chapters explore typical aspects of the faculty career and life cycle—such as appointment, tenure, promotion, incivility, plagiarism, teaching, online delivery, interactions with chairs and deans, and performance appraisal—but examines the prickly issues as well as the routine.

A Faculty Guide for Succeeding in Academe presents authentic, engaging vignettes that feature faculty and administrators as they maneuver through academe encountering difficult situations. Focusing on positive outcomes, each case is analyzed and readers are encouraged to reflect about the ways these incidents could have been resolved. Offering concrete suggestions and best-practices, this book provides insights that will help prospective, new, and current faculty maneuver more effectively through academe and their collegial culture. This important resource enhances a culture of openness and will help faculty gain direction and support in their careers.

Darla J. Twale has coordinated higher education leadership programs and instructed for more than twenty years, including teaching a doctoral course on the professoriate. Formerly on the faculty at Auburn University and the University of Dayton, she has transitioned to teaching online graduated courses and currently teaches as an Adjunct Professor at the University of Pittsburgh, USA.

A Faculty Guide for Succeeding in Academe

Darla J. Twale

Routledge
Taylor & Francis Group
NEW YORK AND LONDON

First published 2013
by Routledge
711 Third Avenue, New York, NY 10017

Simultaneously published in the UK
by Routledge
2 Park Square, Milton Park, Abingdon, Oxon OX14 4RN

Routledge is an imprint of the Taylor & Francis Group, an informa business

© 2013 Taylor & Francis

The right of Darla J. Twale to be identified as author of this work has been asserted by him/her in accordance with sections 77 and 78 of the Copyright, Designs and Patents Act 1988.

All rights reserved. No part of this book may be reprinted or reproduced or utilized in any form or by any electronic, mechanical, or other means, now known or hereafter invented, including photocopying and recording, or in any information storage or retrieval system, without permission in writing from the publishers.

Trademark notice: Product or corporate names may be trademarks or registered trademarks, and are used only for identification and explanation without intent to infringe.

Library of Congress Cataloging in Publication Data
Twale, Darla J. (Darla Jean)
  A faculty guide for succeeding in academe/by Darla J. Twale.
  pages cm
  Includes bibliographical references and index.
  1. College teachers. 2. College teaching. I. Title.
  LB1778.T87 2013
  378.1'2—dc23   2013012110

ISBN: 978-0-415-64451-8 (hbk)
ISBN: 978-0-415-64452-5 (pbk)
ISBN: 978-0-203-07946-1 (ebk)

Typeset in Perpetua and Bell Gothic
by Florence Production Ltd, Stoodleigh, Devon

Printed and bound in the United States of America by Publishers Graphics, LLC on sustainably sourced paper.

To special colleagues, mentors, and administrators who influenced me throughout my career

Paula, Marie, Fran, Patricia, Will, Arlene, and Constance

And for His glory

Contents

	Preface	ix
1	Introduction: The Professoriate, Collegiality, and Academic Culture	1
2	Faculty Search Committees: Finding the Correct Match	9
3	Classroom Teaching and Evaluation	24
4	Teaching Online: Shoot, Aim, Ready	39
5	Departmental Culture: Expect the Unexpected	48
6	On the Tenure Track	57
7	Conferencing and Publishing	76
8	Campus Service and Institutional Citizenship	83
9	Faculty and Administrator Relationships	91
10	Off the Tenure Track *with Janice Epstein*	100
11	Pathways to Full Professor	108
	Epilog	116
	References	120
	Index	131

Preface

Higher education is my life. I spent 11 years getting a BA, two MAs, and a PhD. Years of part-time teaching occurred at the local community college, a regional branch campus of our state flagship university, as well as short stints teaching at two of my alma maters. That was followed by 11 years at Auburn University where I received tenure and eventually promotion to full, 11 at the University of Dayton where I entered full and tenured, one year consulting with the Union Institute and University, and three years and counting in semi-retirement at my last alma mater, Pitt. Through all of this I learned about the faculty role and eventually taught a doctoral course on the professoriate.

Some of my experiences as faculty ranged from highly useful to my career to personally challenging. However, in retrospect, I now see those experiences in a very different light, albeit as great learning experiences, wherever they appeared on my continuum. Thanks to the light that illuminated previously what had been 'under the veil,' I view these experiences in the context of the culture of the collegium. Had I seen them for what they were back in the day, I may have responded differently. Back then, to borrow an analogy, I found myself in the stream, at times treading water, fighting the current, coasting on a raft, fishing and catching more carp than trout, yelling at passing jet-ski riders, dropping anchor, bailing water, and eventually, tying my rope to the semi-retirement dock. After reading A.W. Tozer (2007), I gained more perspective on what I had been experiencing in academe. Using the biblical explanation of the raven launched from Noah's ark, Tozer clarified it for me: "It doesn't seem to bother people at all because they are just as the raven was, at home in their desolation . . . but the woeful thing is we accept it as such instead of being horrified by it" (p. 82) and wanting to make it better. I want academe to be a better place so I decided to share what I learned about being a professor with my peers.

Because my journey was replete with moments of excitement, frustration, *and* fulfillment, an introspective look at the faculty role back then would have been helpful to me. While writing about it seems therapeutic to me now, I hope the information provided here will be beneficial to faculty preparing for the position; those new to the institution; those on *and* off the tenure track; those preparing for tenure and/or promotion; those serving on committees; those presenting and publishing; those teaching online; those contemplating administrative roles; and those highly engaged and those feeling disengaged.

Like me, many incoming faculty learn and stumble as they go. Bringing aspects of our academic trinity to light will help prospective, new, and current faculty maneuver more effectively through academe and their collegial culture. I wrote this book to offer readers insight into the faculty role and what situations they may encounter throughout their careers. Using authentic stories of faculty maneuvering through academe encountering the unexpected, I hope to touch and engage the reader. Explaining what happened to the characters, how they resolved the issues, how theory, research, and practice informed the situations, what best practices may be gleaned from the experiences, and finally, what resources would further enlighten the readers' knowledge of the issues may prevent readers from stumbling.

Although these authentic stories lean toward faculty at research institutions, most of the information should be transferable to new faculty at other institutional classifications. Criteria for inclusion of these stories reflected my knowledge of what issues affect faculty, most of which I gleaned from my scholarly research and reading. My sense is that faculty reading the book will have encountered similar circumstances. Chapters open with an introduction and contain a series of offset sections alerting the reader when they are encountering the case vignettes. I intersperse pertinent scholarship between the italicized vignettes that discuss and debrief topics and, then, offer an explanation for the outcome in each case. Acting as voyeurs, readers examine each character's circumstances viewed from different perspectives as to what could or might have been done. I discuss the final outcome of the cases in order to bring closure to the situations.

In order to understand the faculty role, we must recognize the basic tenets of the academic culture. Therefore, the first chapter addresses the fundamental concepts of academic culture: collegiality, academic freedom, and autonomy. Chapter 1's discussion of the collegium also presents inherent paradoxes associated with it: for instance, whether faculty truly embody the collaborative, relational expectations of collegiality or whether they naturally gravitate to become more autonomous, insular beings because they are tasked with teaching in their individual classrooms and publishing their research. In fact, theorists and researchers question whether autonomy and academic freedom lay the foundation for less collegiality by introducing elements of disengagement and dysfunction into the collegium. Combating the latter, however, should be the goal of faculty peers. From there, we explore aspects of the faculty role and major career rites of passage in the chapters that follow.

Initially the faculty role begins with the search process. Chapter 2 focuses on search committee composition and hiring procedures and how these can affect significantly the culture and the future direction of the department as well as embody the collegial process in action. The characters in this chapter must first, however, understand the collegial culture in which they are working or interviewing.

The next two chapters address the issues associated with classroom and online teaching. Chapter 3 highlights a few issues that faculty tend to avoid sharing with colleagues such as results of their teaching evaluations, incivility, and plagiarism. Silencing matters does little for raising faculty morale or affecting departmental collegiality. Realizing the importance of airing these concerns publically may alter the policy and procedures that currently surround them. With regard to teaching online, faculty discussion often centers on administrative push and faculty resistance. Atypically, Chapter 4 focuses on several faculty who embraced online education but found their efforts thwarted by administrations that entered the online market too soon and failed to support faculty efforts. Both chapters illustrate that faculty members must collaborate with one another and experience mutual cooperation with staff and administrative bodies to allow shared visions to reach fruition.

Chapter 5 exposes the strengths and shortcomings of the faculty home, the academic department. Through faculty meetings, members learn of the power bases and the interplay between them, the degree to which authority figures exert paternalism, and the extent to which colleagues act collegially. Over the faculty member's next several years, he or she will assess his or her potential fit in the department. In Chapter 6, faculty read about the various steps to tenure and promotion to associate including pre-tenure review and graduate faculty status and how to avoid potential politics and missteps.

Attending conferences to present research and eventually getting that scholarship published in peer-reviewed journals keeps faculty engaged. In the context of exercising academic freedom and autonomy, Chapter 7 examines the importance of scholarship and the ethical expectations surrounding it. While teaching and research occupy the bulk of the professor's job, faculty also fulfill a service function. Chapter 8 offers insight into the expectation for good institutional citizenship without the benefit of solid, explicit guidelines for performing or measuring it. The focus centers on the alignment of teaching, research, and service duties to facilitate a tighter career agenda that assists faculty with gaining tenure and promotion.

While the previous chapters address faculty working with faculty, Chapter 9 explores faculty interface with administrators, specifically chairs/heads and deans, and shows that differences in perception may determine how they react to one another. To further illustrate that point between faculty and administration,

PREFACE

Chapter 10 chronicles the tumultuous relationship between a non-tenure track employee and various supervisors and faculty colleagues. While the situations strained relationships and challenged grievance procedures, the outcome ignited a fire that enlightened a campus.

Chapter 11 focuses on mid-career faculty who set their sights on achieving promotion to full professor. Faculty success in achieving this goal rests firmly on defined career plans, continued professional development, clearly articulated promotion guidelines, and the minimization of internal political obstacles. Perhaps that accounts for fewer incumbents in this role. To conclude, the Epilog summarizes the book through the eyes of two colleagues who shared an early career journey. Each chose a different path but with their shared insights, knowledge of the collegial culture, and effective use of the information they acquired, both experienced successful academic careers.

Using the many vignettes to illustrate my points, I offer in this book a realistic view of the professoriate, the collegium, and the academic culture. In lieu of the introspective book I wish someone else had penned and I had the time to read 30 years ago, this academic retrospective sheds light for every novice just beginning his or her journey as well as for all the seasoned faculty scholars who continue to trek diligently on their academic paths.

Please note that in all case studies, pseudonyms have been used.

Darla J. Twale
November 2012

Everything exposed by the light becomes visible . . .

Ephesians 5:14(NIV)

Chapter 1
Introduction
The Professoriate, Collegiality, and Academic Culture

Outsiders to academic culture read or see images of professors portrayed in books and on screen. Whether they recall the shy, beloved, inspiring Mr. Chips or the scholarly but engrossed, absent-minded professor, they see stereotypes and linear tasks rather than the complicated, overlapping roles of a typical member of the collegium. On the fringes, we hear of the occasional eccentric, weird, mad scientist attempting to create a deadly virus that will destroy an entire society or his or her persistent counterpart who strives to devise the antidote to it. Media coverage depicted the professor for whom the stress of academic life became so overwhelming that she killed and wounded colleagues whom she believed blocked her tenure. An award-winning movie based on the life of John Nash illustrated the academic world of an asocial, disillusioned, obsessive, although Nobel Prize winning, professor (Howard, 2001). Professor Higgins used his fictional skills to illustrate how tutoring affects teaching and learning outcomes on a student, Eliza Doolittle. These familiar examples span the gamut of faculty stereotypes, but few truly or totally depict academic reality.

For those of us with years of experience in academe, we see and perhaps embody a few eccentric characteristics, but mostly we tend to be hard-working members of staff who prepare and teach interesting classes, advise and supervise graduate and undergraduate students, engage in cutting-edge research, publish in scholarly and practitioner journals, and serve on committees both at the institutional level and in our professional fields. Occasionally, we encounter colleagues who have become deadwood, others who are obviously disengaged from their departments, and others likely to leave the institution seeking a better fit elsewhere. We work with a few pompous colleagues as well as the self-promoters who tend to pad their accomplishments or overstate their significance. We tolerate a few cynical colleagues who strike down good ideas because they did not work when others suggested those ideas 20 years ago. Even a prima donna or two may demand star billing, an office with a window, and a better parking space. But largely, we characterize ourselves as a collection of committed educators who enjoy being part of a true community of scholars. Sometimes we are fortunate to achieve that community feeling but unfortunately not always and not for extended periods of time. Our desire to be collegial may take a back seat to our individual preoccupation with tenure and promotion. And, we find ourselves currently competing for scarce resources that with each passing year become even scarcer.

All stereotypes aside, faculty perform a multiplicity of complicated roles. That list, in no particular order, includes professor/teacher, researcher, advisor, evaluator, committee member and/or chair, quasi-administrator, writer, editor, reader, thesis/dissertation supervisor, curriculum planner, presenter, discussant, author, change agent, intellectual, ethicist, monitor, learner, reviewer, examiner, and gate-keeper. Note that this list does not take into consideration those in the hard sciences and hard applied sciences who experiment, discover, and oversee labs. Nor does it include all of the professoriate who has had to move beyond chalk and erasers to master the technical aspects of instructional delivery in a state-of-the-art classroom or in an online format. Because of the diversity associated with the faculty role and its expectations and obligations, the role will become more, rather than less, complex in the future. It is no wonder that faculty stresses and challenges affect faculty culture and collegiality (Buckholdt & Miller, 2009). So, let's address these situations in order that we may cope with scarcer resources, hectic schedules, extreme personalities, odd policies, and the often overwhelming expectations for success.

FACULTY ROLE OBLIGATIONS

Edward Shils (1997) considered faculty to have several obligations during an academic appointment. Their first and most basic obligation rested on knowing and sustaining their field/discipline within academe. To fulfill that obligation meant making the proper academic appointments of highly capable junior and senior scholars. It should be the cherished role of faculty to search for, vet, interview, and recommend to the chair and/or dean new faculty members to the department. Populating that pool of prospective candidates means that graduate faculty must carefully instruct, mentor, advise, and guide graduate students and their research. Responsibility for the next generation of scholars remains an awesome task for seasoned faculty.

Shils (1997) maintained that the second faculty obligation to the university and the collegium is the search for truth. Truth is obtained through teaching the truth to students and striving for truth through faculty research and publication. Searching for the truth through new discovery characterizes the "life of the mind," or the academic life. Shils cautioned faculty to never lose sight of this second obligation and also reminded faculty of their ethical duties as professionals. He cautioned, however, that resources, politics, students, and stakeholder scrutiny in academe has changed. As such, Shils opined that "the self-confidence of the academic profession in its devotion to its calling has faltered" (p. 7). He offered several reasons: the separation of faculty grouped into academic departments on campus and as members of academic and professional societies associated with their disciplines or fields off campus. Too often faculty loyalty lies within their discipline/field rather than their institution (Gouldner, 1958). We evidence this when we consider that each professor owns the means of production at his or her institution through the acquisition of expert knowledge in a particular field. This forces faculty to uphold ethical standards that Shils confirmed is faculty's third obligation. Faculty must maintain high ethical standards through "the pursuit and transmission of advanced knowledge" and through the "conduct affected by the real or presumed possession of such knowledge" (p. 9). How faculty must do this, that is the degree to which they practice collegiality, affects the functioning of the collegium and the prevailing academic culture.

COLLEGIALITY, COLLEGIAL CULTURE, AND THE COLLEGIUM

Although Orlans (2002) contended that collegiality seemed too vague to characterize, Bennett (1998) defined the term earlier as "participation in the academic life of an institution," which "requires intellectual reciprocity with colleagues and . . . an openness beyond the collegium" (p. 125). By nature, the collegium is relational, committed, connected, associational, and functional. The collegium is faculty's intellectual sanctuary. Ideally, collegiality flourishes where colleagues interact, treat one another with respect, and exchange intellectual thoughts (Diamond, 2002). Collective effort must be forthcoming from departmental members if the organization is to move forward. Faculty must prove to be good citizens with regard to accepting responsibility for departmental, college, and university tasks, using their expertise to propose solutions to problems, continually striving for environmental improvement, and representing the institution and their profession well (Diamond, 2002). Without collective effort coupled with more faculty tendency toward personal isolation and insulation, the schoolhouse door swings open to dysfunction, disengagement, fragmentation, pomposity, incivility, alienation, and eventual destruction of the true collegium. Bennett added that balancing isolation with community appears necessary for a relational collegium to flourish.

Bennett (1998) referred to interaction and discourse as the means to facilitate a relational collegium. Because peer review is a defining aspect of the collegium, it should be embraced to advance a healthy organization, especially considering that power is unevenly distributed throughout the collegium. Bennett advocated that "acceptance and critical judgment require interest in the work of others, and that in turn, means knowledge of, and a modicum of care for, the well-being and growth of others" (p. 33). However, the collegial culture places emphasis on "powerful competition and striving for prestige and dominance" (Bergquist & Pawlak, 2008, p. 33). Bergquist and Pawlak's notion of the collegial culture is not depicted in a typical campus organizational chart because autonomy and academic freedom form the normative structure of the collegial culture, not lines and positions. As a result, Campbell (2000) reminded us that "the folkways that reinforce ingrained practice in the academic ivory tower are tenaciously held and zealously protected" (p. 161) regardless of what they are.

Faculty departments have been labeled nation-states by Bennett (1998) and powerful fiefdoms by Bergquist and Pawlak (2008). Institutions, generally, and departments, specifically, determine the extent to which teaching, research, or service takes precedent. Expectations for tenure and promotion could differ from one department to another despite the common document by which all faculty in an institution abides. For instance the collegium espouses collaboration among its members but expects faculty to develop personal research agendas and publish articles as sole authorships (Knight, 2010).

Outsiders to academe may describe the collegium as homogeneous and homosocial, but it is more like a heterocosm. Because departmental faculty is grouped by discipline and field, the members tend to be homogeneous. This may flow from the fact that faculty, through the practice of homosocial reproduction, hire their own colleagues and tend to interview and extend invitations to persons whom they believe are *like* them, fit into their existing departmental culture, and perhaps have similar research interests. The collegium on the one hand mirrors and reproduces itself while on the other hand it opposes actions associated with it (i.e., heterocosm). Ironically, the collegium often reproduces the very features it purports to oppose because of its conservative nature (Damrosch, 1995).

Academic values associated with the collegial culture seem to be overshadowed by corporate values and market strategies. Of late, business and corporate models run more of higher education than collegial values once did. Some faculty shifted sides to become more entrepreneurial. Washburn (2005) expanded her argument by saying, "It appears that money has blinded most universities to this rather obvious inconsistency in commercial versus academic aims" (p. 161). In job-shop fashion, the university, she anticipates, will do anything for money, prestige, visibility, and/or viability. And, unfortunately, she contended that some faculty and administrations have succumbed to this mentality and, as a result, the collegium has become something that it probably once reviled. While the current collegium may not be the collegium of old, it does need to anticipate change and deal accordingly. Pendulums continue to swing and the collegium must continue to adapt.

At odds with the collegium is the entrepreneurial-focused, administratively powered managerial culture (Bergquist & Pawlak, 2008). For this culture, accountability, strategic planning, efficiency, and fiscal responsibility reigns sovereign. Balance and creative tension between management/administration and the collegial culture means the academic department, school, or college must remain functional. Imbalance between the two cultures leads to a dysfunctional environment and the concomitant rise of a political or advocacy culture formed to address faculty disenfranchisement. The last thing an administration desires is the contempt of the faculty because it implemented new policies that infringe on the time that faculty have to devote to research and teaching (Bergquist & Pawlak, 2008; Senge, 1990). Cahn (1994) wrote, because "the proper role of faculty members is to guide the learning process, their authority to do so must be respected and protected" (p. 38). However, savvy faculty leaders can masterfully thwart any managerial plan laid out by their department head or dean that infringes on their comfortable collegial culture (Burgan, 2006) which may not always be productive for the organization.

Because the academy tends toward conservatism, it typically resists change. Questioning the status quo signals a move toward progress. However, some faculty remain silent and allow outdated methods or informal mores to perpetuate. The worst the senior faculty can do is "hide and obscure" the reality of the organization and culture from incumbents as well as novices (Bennett, 1998, p. 33). Acts of hiding and obscuring force resistance to new ideas, especially those introduced by the newer members to the collegium. Poor socialization and enculturation into a department may hinder a true community of scholars from forming. Resulting isolation and individuation promote self-aggrandizement that runs counter to the tenets of the collegium (Cahn, 1994; Cipriano, 2011; Palmer, 1998). Awareness of these trends is important for those preparing to enter academe as well as those mentoring them.

Virtual and entrepreneurial growth allows the university a competitive advantage with business, industry, and other institutions. While administrators view the online option as a cost-effective strategy in the long term, some faculty believe that online delivery challenges the traditional collegium and value of the institution. Intangible or virtual campuses, some believe, dissolve the traditions, values, and symbols associated with the tangible campus and erode the conservative collegial culture (Bergquist & Pawlak, 2008; Burgan, 2006). Faculty may feel that this is yet another example of what Campbell (2000) referred to as marketing for the cash cow. Faculty challenge the educational benefits of online delivery on the basis that the use of adjunct and part-time faculty shows the medium to be more cost-effective rather than emphasizing excellence and quality of instructional delivery. Other faculty would argue that online delivery when done correctly can be as good as or better than what students receive from the tangible classroom. All this speaks to the nature of the collegium and the effort to preserve the collegial culture and its community of scholars.

INTRODUCTION

PARADOXES AND IRONIES WITHIN THE COLLEGIUM

Douglas (1986) wrote about the irony associated with institutions of higher education. She said, "Institutions create shadowed places in which nothing can be seen and no questions asked" but, ironically, these same institutions "make other areas show finely discriminated detail, which is closely scrutinized and ordered" (p. 69). Lang (2005) referred to "undercurrents of departmental intrigue," which extends Douglas' notion of a purposefully hidden nature of academe (p. 109). Paradoxically, the search for knowledge and the quest for new discovery associated with the collegium run counter to this picture of academe and the hope that openness always prevails.

Although we presume the collegium to be a collectivity, Bennett (2000) argued the contrary. Collegiums should be aggregates bound by covenant not contract. That covenant becomes the means by which peers both offer civil critique and, likewise, listen and process information. Like a church body, the academy members come blessed with diverse gifts by which they contribute to the whole body, and ideally, support its functioning. As a collective and because faculty members are agents both of change and continuity, the whole is greater than any one member alone can claim. Inevitably, the collective sustains fluidity and growth to remain dynamic as opposed to static; covenants facilitate this better than contracts, Bennett contended.

Palmer (1998) noticed that faculty conceal aspects of themselves from one another. To avoid what Palmer referred to as live encounters, faculty may hide behind their credentials, academic specialties, research prowess, and their *perceived* power in the academy. Openly challenging peers appears to be one thing faculty avoid. Faculty tend to maintain social distance. Faculty tend not to speak out against anyone. As a result faculty may allow poor habits to form, to solidify, or to become engrained, preferring to remain silent, indifferent, or aloof (Bennett, 1998; Washburn, 2005). This runs counter to faculty's searching for and speaking the truth.

Burton Clark (1987, p. 140) realized that faculty working in their departments appear only to strive for "symbolic integration." They are together as a corporate body physically but often are leading isolated lives moving from classroom to classroom, lab to lab, laptop to laptop, and often researching in a specialty shared by no one else in their department. What may resemble corporate culture or a collegium is merely a façade for the more engrained subcultures and silos. Furthermore, conferences and association meetings create forums for fellow scholars to present their research and to receive critique in a language only they seem to understand (Bennett, 1998). Academe further separates itself from the outside world and in most instances from one another. In some departments the subcultures may not speak the same language or, if they do, will not always be listening or on speaking terms!

The collegium tends to perpetuate the status quo and current climate regardless of how well it functions. Tasked to pursue, discover, and uncover the truth, faculty can inadvertently as well as purposefully stifle, evade, overlook, and ignore issues, observations, and encounters within academe. Engaging in both sets of behaviors affects the role faculty play; that is, professors, researchers, committee members, and disciplinary professionals. More importantly, it shapes how faculty socialize and mentor the next generation of graduate students who enter their professorial ranks (Slevin, 1993). Academic socialization and enculturation tend to be as to fit the 'spirit' of the situation as much as the reality of it.

Shils (1997) acknowledged that academe may be "in danger of discredit" (p. 10). The two basic faculty privileges—academic freedom and autonomy—may be the reasons because of the challenges they engender from inside and outside stakeholders in higher education. These two academic privileges come with obligations, accountability, fiduciary responsibility, and codes of ethics that must be addressed (Barrow & Keeney, 2006). In fact, academic freedom endues faculty to be morally obliged to uphold the academic freedom of their colleagues (De George, 2003). De George added that our academic forefathers encouraged academic freedom not to protect individual members of the academy but rather to protect society by encouraging the academy's search for truth and its subsequent dissemination.

Another reason for the 'danger of discredit' may be that some faculty members have "lost their zeal and . . . fall short of the [professional] standards which they know ought to prevail" (Shils, 1997, p. 12). Increasing that zeal, raising morale, and enhancing faculty engagement should be of utmost concern to faculty and those who develop faculty and administrate faculty affairs.

As faculties grow larger, they splinter into specialty groups, compete for scarcer resources, and often tend to isolate themselves. Of late, we have witnessed a decrease in tenure track positions and more online offerings, which concomitantly decrease *perceived* opportunities for intellectual collectivities and communities of scholars on campus. Reybold (2008) acknowledged an integrity crisis among faculty in higher education: falsified job applications; poor faculty preparation for classroom lectures; rubber-stamped, ungraded term papers; breeched confidentiality; and fabricated research data. Evidence of exploitation, workplace harassment, discrimination, and intolerance increases in academe rather than decreases (Namie & Namie, 2000; Twale & De Luca, 2008). Documented behaviors listed above occur between faculty colleagues, faculty and students, and faculty and administration. Reybold reminded faculty that they "are obligated to the community of scholars, particularly with respect to collegial interactions and shared governance" (2008, p. 281). However, competition, isolation, and stress render some faculty unable to fulfill these expectations. Faculty need to address collegiality and integrity issues and recapture the community of scholars' perspective.

INTRODUCTION

Faculty face tasks throughout their career including their first interview and eventual hiring, teaching students, attending faculty meetings, developing a research agenda, presenting at conferences, working with colleagues and students, submitting manuscripts, getting published, going up for tenure, interacting with administrators, and eventually going up for full professor. Experience teaches faculty that some events will pass as expected but others will completely shock and surprise them. The following chapters capture the pleasant and unpleasant surprises, major catastrophes, and minor subtleties for which we do not anticipate and for which we are not prepared to handle. As newcomers pass through these many faculty rites of passage, they can benefit from the experiences of those who have traversed before them. How they handled the situation can provide others with support, direction, practical advice, and inspiration as how to address similar situations. Let's begin at the beginning, the faculty search process.

Chapter 2

Faculty Search Committees

Finding the Correct Match

INTRODUCTION

Newly hired faculty experience the hiring side of the search committee process. But, at some point, all faculty will serve on a search committee. The process entails CVs, phone interviews, on-campus interviews, calls from the dean or department chair, and unfortunately, writing or receiving the rejection letter. The ultimate search committee goal seems to be to find a good 'fit' for the department (academic). Faculty also tends to look for someone who 'fits in' with the rest of the department (social, personal). Arguments for and against these guidelines of homosocial reproduction tend to create either insular or homogeneous departments. On the other hand, if the candidate fits in, he or she most likely will stay and the department will forego another expensive and time-consuming search in the near future (Landrum & Clump, 2004).

Search committee composition raises issues initially as to who should serve on a search committee based on rank and tenure. In addition, different personalities possess the ability to drive the committee in a direction or allow it to coast on its own (Simplicio, 2007). As a department head/chair identifies search committee members, he or she needs to show the greatest concern for appointing informed and conscientious members (Landrum & Clump, 2004) rather than faculty members who demonstrate a cavalier or disinterested approach. Some faculty members also possess the power and political leverage to maneuver the search to meet their goals, which may or may not be aligned with departmental or college goals.

Sifting through stacks of CVs, vetting candidates, and calling references takes precious faculty time (Cohen, 2004; Gilreath, Foster, Reynolds, & Tucker, 2009; Landrum & Clump, 2004) but is time well spent in service to the department or college and the professional area. Coordinating faculty and student schedules so that the majority of departmental members can speak to the candidate(s) and attend his or her presentation can be exhausting. Interviews allow the faculty and staff to court candidates and for the candidate to determine if this position, institution, department, and faculty are compatible with one another. In other words, it becomes a "delicate ballet of negotiations" where each faction evaluates the other (Herreid & Full, 2010, p. 12).

The search process, however, can be one of the best depictions of collegiality. Faculty must work together as a team to compose the ad, examine the pool, vet the top candidates, express expectations to the candidate, court top selections, present colleagues at their best, sell the department's positive characteristics, and minimize the less than attractive features. Even dysfunctional departments must exhibit some level of functionality. Disengaged or dissatisfied faculty members must struggle to be positive about the institution when they interview candidates. Candidates engage in creating the same façade to impress the search committee— wearing his best suit and putting her best foot forward. The following vignettes address search committee composition and the vetting process.

New Assistant Professor—Good Opportunity to be the Search Committee Chair?

In her second year as an assistant professor, Nancy found herself in a precarious position. Her soon-to-retire department head, Tom, asked her to chair a large search committee. One committee would oversee the quest to fill five positions and consist of representatives from all program areas in the department. Tom assured her that this would be a wonderful opportunity and experience for her, helping her work with faculty in the department and showing her how the department functioned. More importantly, Tom added, this would count toward her tenure. Being a bit suspicious, Nancy decided to think it over for a few days and would get back to Tom. She immediately called her respected and untenured colleague, Barb, to relay the news.

Not surprised by the department head's offer, Barb expressed disdain that Tom would even think of asking a relatively new, untenured professor to assume such an auspicious and politically charged position. Barb and Nancy speculated as to Tom's motives for asking her in the first place. They also discussed repercussions that might transpire if Nancy turned down the post. So, Barb and Nancy brainstormed in order to determine the best approach for Nancy to take when she reported back to Tom.

Nancy's colleague, Barb, suspected Tom's scheme and talked Nancy successfully out of falling for it. She thought Nancy should probably turn down any involvement with the search but Nancy and she realized that the repercussions might be worse than serving. Neither woman could predict what new scheme Tom might dream up. They needed to be one step ahead of him.

On Monday morning, Nancy informed Tom that she would be happy to serve on the search committee but not as chair. Appearing somewhat disappointed by the decision, Tom placed his best friend, Mike, as committee chair and agreed to let Nancy serve on the committee. On a hunch, Nancy decided to ask Mike about the potential workload for the search committee chair. Mike informed Nancy that several departmental secretaries covered all the administrative tasks like scheduling, coordinating, and facilitating the on-campus interviews, dinners, and presentations. Mike intended to chair meetings and vet candidates only. Odd, when Tom offered the position to Nancy, he failed to mention this support. Tom led Nancy to believe she would be taking care of all that detail.

Was that an oversight or did Tom hope that Nancy would take on those additional clerical tasks herself? Nancy presumed she would be taking on a great deal of responsibility had she accepted the chair position but it appears that Mike took on very little. He delegated most of the work to the committee members and the rest fell on the departmental secretaries. Knowing that bit of information might have altered Nancy's final decision but then again she rationalized that perhaps the same services would not have been offered to her as they were to Tom's best friend, Mike.

This department head ran a relaxed ship, privy to the whims of Tom's long-time friends and old buddies like Mike. The presence of new female faculty challenged Tom's long-standing values and his perception of what the department and field had been and, thus, should be. As the gender tide shifted in the department, Tom considered placing a new, naïve female faculty member as chair of a search committee. Perhaps, he believed, she would be overwhelmed and she would run screaming out of the university. He could have selected another tenured female but Nancy probably struck him as the most likely to fall for the con. Clearly Barb could have been a candidate but she must have appeared a bit too savvy for Tom to have offered her the position.

As department head and departmental member for 30 years, Tom had to know that search committee chairs *should* be tenured faculty members who hold senior rather than junior status. Nancy, only in her second year at the university, knew little about the campus or the surrounding city to be of true assistance to any interviewing candidate. Nancy might encounter difficulty responding to candidate questions about the department, programs, or city, for instance. Candidates might also wonder why someone so new to the department was given and assumed this level of responsibility. Nancy's current focus should revolve around class preparations and carrying out her newly fashioned research agenda. To be bothered with such service obligations at this point in her career, especially one as daunting as this, would be ill-advised for any novice.

Red flags went up for Nancy and Barb when the search encompassed five positions at once. What was wrong with this picture, they pondered? With Barb's guidance, Nancy brainstormed why Tom asked her to be chair: She probably threatened his position by being ambitious and hard-working. His laissez-faire management style complemented his research agenda as he had not published in decades. Tom tried to railroad Nancy, paint a rosy though inaccurate picture to her, and lure her into a no-win situation, possibly taking her off track for tenure.

Leveraging the Search for Personal Gain?

Three top candidates emerged from a pile of 30 CVs. As was the policy, the department would bring in the top candidate first and if the faculty and the candidate proved to be a match and the candidate accepted the offer extended, the search would be closed. Carl chaired the committee. Committee members decided to court their top selection, an untenured minority male from a top research institution who had four years' experience. Carl became puzzled as to why this candidate would want to leave such a fine program for one of lesser quality. During the visit, the candidate, George, presented his research quite well, impressed the search committee, and captivated the faculty and graduate students with whom he interviewed. Following the visit, the faculty met to discuss whether or not to offer George the position.

Anticipating that the vote would be unanimous, and the meeting therefore extremely short, the faculty sat awestruck when Carl offered his insights. No other faculty corroborated Carl's perceptions. In his one-on-one with George, Carl gleaned that George gave evidence of insincerity. Carl tried to convince his colleagues in the meeting that George's responses seemed evasive and, often, too rehearsed. Carl did not get a sense that George was truly interested in joining the program. In addition, Carl mentioned that in his previous position outside academe, he interviewed many candidates and his gut told him that George had an agenda. Carl speculated that George probably wanted a raise from his current institution and used this job search as leverage to secure it. Nonetheless Carl failed to sway the faculty as they voted 13 to 1 in favor of offering George the position. The department chair relayed to the dean the recommendation to offer George the position and then called George with the good news. George asked for a few days to think it over.

While this position had been unfilled for two years, the dean announced that the inability to fill it this time would mean the loss of the position to that program. No one in the department wanted that to happen. Even though the committee indeed selected the best applicant to interview, they believed they would convince this candidate to leave his program for theirs. Not only did George ideally fit the faculty opening, he represented a minority. As visions of sugar plums danced in the search committee's heads, the department faculty may have been as eager to hire George as they were for the anticipated 'new' faculty position—perhaps, even more so. That could explain why Carl's assessment of George fell on deaf ears. Days after the interview, George informed the department chair that his nationally recognized institution had made him a counter offer and he had decided to remain at his current institution.

Forcing faculty to hire someone or lose a faculty position amounts to administrative blackmail. Had the committee selected a strong candidate other than George, and not from a nationally recognized program, perhaps the search would have been different. But, you go with the candidate who bubbles to the top. But the administration dangled another carrot to the department when it learned that the top choice represented a minority group: If the department hired a minority candidate, then another faculty position would open up in the department.

Because the faculty or the committee specifically had no way of knowing George's motives, they must all presume those intentions were honorable. Carl alleged that they were less than honorable. Carl argued that George played the system for George's own personal gain. The faculty, however, witnessed a very personable candidate who interviewed well. George would have the faculty believe that he wanted to leave his nationally acclaimed program for opportunities in another program that was fine, but not nationally recognized. Carl used his expertise and considerable experience as an interviewer to reach the conclusion that George exhibited insincerity and a somewhat cavalier attitude. In trying to convince his colleagues of George's insincerity, Carl flunked miserably.

Well respected by his colleagues, Carl wondered why they failed to acknowledge *his* expertise or see *his* point of view. Carl may have taken pleasure in knowing that his perceptions had not forsaken him but few colleagues acknowledged his insightful ability. Carl knew that their stance during the meeting probably stemmed from the dangling carrot as well as the false impression George made. His colleagues' perceptions troubled him.

Internal Department Chair Search

As is typical, when a department head is promoted, departs, or retires, an internal rather than an external search is conducted for a new head. In this merged department, three candidates, all from the same program, indicated their willingness to serve as department head. The three candidates were tenured full professors. The search committee consisted of one person from each of the three program areas. All were tenured, associate professors, and well-respected members of the department.

Each of the candidates interviewed with the search committee for an hour and each was asked the critical question of why he or she wanted to be the new department head. Female candidate, Liz, stunned the panel when she responded that she planned to retire in three years and this would increase her social security and retirement benefits as her salary would be larger. Years earlier Liz had held a one-year interim chair position so she had experience. Male candidate, Bill, surprised the committee when he stated that they knew him well enough to form their own opinion. In other words, the panel would know that he was the type of person that would make a better department head than the other two candidates. Male candidate, Norm, had clearly done his homework and responded with his plans to assist the department faculty and its programs and to raise departmental standards to ensure continued quality and performance.

Deliberations by the three-member search panel ended quickly. They brought their recommendation to the faculty who sat befuddled at their suggestion and reasoning but who acquiesced because they respected their judgment. The panel recommended to

FACULTY SEARCH COMMITTEES

the dean that Norm become the new department head. Because the dean knew Liz and Bill much better, he had been looking forward to working with one of them. So he reluctantly accepted the committee's recommendation and offered the position to Norm.

Situated in his new position, Norm failed to implement any of his stated plans, much to the dismay of the search committee, his colleagues, and the dean. As the deflated balloon quickly hit the floor and dashed the hopes of the faculty, Norm quietly moved into his spacious corner office, shut the door, and continued to work on his research agenda.

Search committee selection appeared to be appropriate in this situation. To recommend a candidate for chair, search members must be tenured. Ideally, they would have been at the full level but that is not always possible. Two of the three members also held quasi-administrative positions in their program areas. All three held the respect of their colleagues. Each committee member knew the three candidates enough time to make an informed decision. Search committee members expected each candidate to make a presentation of their vision and strategic plan for the department. Only Norm came prepared.

Liz's and Bill's presentations indicated to the committee, however, that they felt the 'who you know' would be more important than 'what you know.' Their preparation for the interview translated to an afterthought, an insignificant moment in the search process, and an impingement on their time. Knowing the candidates and their future needs would be enough to seal the deal, thought Liz and Bill. Each presumed they would be ideal for the position. They knew colleagues liked and respected them. Both focused more on their personal needs, rather than focusing on the department because neither prepared themselves to discuss their vision or strategic plan initiatives with their colleagues.

Norm happened to be the outsider with fewer years of experience on this faculty. However, faculty respected his scholarship. He tended to be more focused on his research than his teaching, however. But, given that this was a research institution, he performed up to the university's expectation of him. As the third person to interview, he possessed the advantage. Perhaps he knew that his colleagues would allow their candidacy to rest on their laurels. Norm did not feel he had that luxury. He chose a different route and prepared his vision and strategic plan following the committee's directive. It worked perfectly.

Giving credence to the dean, could we blame him for wanting to work with known commodities like Liz and Bill? But, the dean kept an open mind as he accepted the recommendation of the search committee and elevated Norm to department head. Surely the department faculty sat stunned at the outcome expecting that Liz or Bill would be given the honor. When the search committee informed the faculty that Norm followed the committee's directive and offered a viable vision and strategic plan for the department, the department faculty shifted their thinking, albeit reluctantly, in anticipation of the implementation of Norm's stated plan. Expecting Liz or Bill as department head but installing Norm instead would surely change their expectations for the department as well as cause them to wonder how the dynamics would play out.

Norm's craftiness fooled the search committee. His salary increased while his teaching workload decreased as he taught less. Furthermore, he chose not to facilitate any of his administrative promises. Now that the faculty realized they had been bamboozled, an 'us' versus 'them' dynamic commenced.

External Search with an Internal Candidate

Russell served as the interim department head for a year while a search committee commenced the search for a permanent replacement. While the pool of candidates was extensive, it was not rich. Two candidates emerged, one man and one woman, and courtesy was extended to Russell as interim. Subsequently, the committee scheduled on-campus interviews with these two men and one woman. During the search, the woman withdrew in order to accept a position elsewhere. Russell and Scott interviewed with the five-member faculty search committee.

Russell's service as chair proved less than stellar and the dean knew it, too. But in the faculty meeting designed to discuss the candidates, the dean noticed that the untenured faculty sat silently. He relayed that fact to the provost. Concerned, the provost called each untenured faculty member in the department that evening at their homes to allow each of them to privately and confidentially air their perceptions of Russell and Scott. When the call came to Helen's home that evening, she was stunned that the provost had called her, a third year untenured professor, to ask what she thought. He encouraged her to be open and honest with her assessment of each candidate. Assuring her of confidentiality, he also convinced Helen that he cared about new faculty to the university: "If we hired the wrong candidate for the wrong reasons, new and promising faculty would likely disengage or depart for other institutions." Helen replied as honestly as she could in the collegial spirit that illuminated the superior qualities of one candidate without demeaning the lesser of the two candidates. The next day other untenured departmental faculty buzzed about their phone calls the previous evening. None of them had expected that a provost would contact untenured faculty to inquire about their perceptions and opinions. He listened, too, making it not a pro forma action but a sincere gesture on his part.

In a few days the dean announced that Scott, the outside candidate, accepted the position much to Russell's dismay. Based on the faculty meeting in which the untenured remained silent, it became clear that Russell had only a few supporters among the tenured faculty. Most favored the unknown to the known commodity. As to what Russell realized regarding why he did not secure the department head position remains to be determined. Knowing Russell, it is likely that he believed most of the faculty caused his downfall. He probably did not realize that his inability to maintain the position rested on his own actions while chair and his lack of a plan for the future.

For an administrator to take this much interest is probably highly unusual, but also highly commendable. The dean should have also been involved but perhaps the provost felt that the new faculty would not be as candid with their dean as they would be with the provost. Untenured faculty likely viewed the candidates from a different vantage point than their tenured colleagues. Both points need to be shared and considered for the future good of the department.

Experienced Hire and the Department Chair

In a much anticipated interview at a fine university, Amy struggled with the material she would use for her presentation. Several days before the interview, she taught a very interesting class on codes of ethics and ethical behavior in her profession. Because that class went so well, she felt comfortable repeating that lesson during her presentation attended by the search committee and a few faculty and students. In attendance was the department chair, Harry, whom Amy had met with earlier. That one-on-one meeting went well, she thought. Harry seemed personable and informative. However, during her presentation, Harry turned his seat around to visibly face another part of the room instead of facing Amy. How rude, she thought. The rest of those in attendance appeared to appreciate the presentation as evidenced by their engagement in the mock class discussion. During most of the presentation, Harry drummed his fingers on the table in apparent disgust. Puzzled, Amy wondered if it was an attempt to throw her off. She knew the rest of the attendees had to take note of his behavior.

In a later meeting with the department chair before she dashed off to the airport, Harry's demeanor had changed from their earlier meeting to parallel the impolite behavior he demonstrated during her presentation. What appeared a positive experience had turned sour. Amy left the campus perplexed. She did expect an offer, but she was also not sure if she wanted one.

Amy received her rejection letter a week later with a note indicating the search would be reopened and the process continued. Three years later Amy attended an annual regional conference and encountered a presenter in a session from the same department in which she had interviewed years earlier. The session presenter, Rick, remembered Amy. She felt compelled to ask him about the failed search. Rick informed Amy that Harry had 'resigned' from his duties a couple of years ago when the administration discovered that he had falsified his credentials in order to obtain the chair position. Amy reasoned that the last thing Harry needed on his faculty was a colleague well versed in ethics. Perhaps, during her presentation, she had even used an example to illustrate her point that mirrored Harry's indiscretions. Amy could not help but wonder what happened to Harry.

Typically the department chair is not the search committee chair because the faculty committee make their recommendation to the administration. To think that the chair had major input into the decision-making process may be a false assumption. The department chair is but one voice among many because the search committee and faculty carry more weight. Should Amy have contacted the search committee chair later to express her concerns for the department chair's discourteous behavior and altered tone toward her? Perhaps, but it could be construed as a touchy situation. What is the real protocol in these instances? Surely there were enough people in attendance to convey displeasure or concern to committee members for Amy about Harry's poor behavior. If the search committee chair knew of Amy's concerns, what would he or she do with the information? Would it make a difference? Because the department chair treated her shabbily, it may be unwise for her to accept a position there anyway, if one was offered.

If the goal is to sell the program, department, and university to a prospective candidate, then the search committee assumes that everyone will be on their best behavior. In this case, Harry clearly neglected to completely sell his department during Amy's presentation. He did during the initial meeting but, during subsequent interactions, obviously, he did not. Something derailed the situation and Amy knew she would be the loser in the long run; therefore, expressing her concern regarding Harry's behavior eventually became a moot point.

DEBRIEFING THE SEARCH COMMITTEE PROCESS

The preceding five vignettes broadly illustrate search committee scenarios and raise issues that involve ethical elements and protocol. Each offers food for thought from the perspective of the candidate, the committee, and the administration. Departmental hiring may be subjected to limited budgets that necessitate internal hires or interviews with a limited pool of external candidates. Often ads ask for someone who probably does not exist. However, external candidates may be encouraged to 'clean house,' implement change, shift direction, or shake up a complacent department (Simplicio, 2007).

The process begins with the dean's authorization to search. However, department chairs along with faculty can manipulate the search process by determining who sits on the committee, the words in the ad, where the ad is published, and ultimately how the committee ranks candidates based on the committee's individual and collective interpretation of what the department needs (Kekes, 1996). Furthermore, the committee's ranking can be influenced by their "prejudices, preferences, personal sympathies and antipathies, extra-institutional loyalties of members of the search committee" (Kekes, 1996, p. 568). Faculty on and off the committee may be swayed during the interview by "the personality, appearance, and attitude of the candidate" (Kekes, 1996, p. 568) as Carl illustrated.

Howze (2008) questioned if search committees evaluated the pool of candidates objectively or scientifically or used some subjective criteria, and concluded that there is no set rationale for what faculty look for in candidates' CVs. Some search committees look to see who served as the candidate's dissertation chair and if that person provided a good reference. Other faculty tend to be swayed by the institution that conferred the doctoral degree. Many hope for someone who has established his or her research agenda and perhaps published an article or two. Faculty often evaluate the candidate as being likeable, that is, settling for congenial rather than searching for collegial compatibility with members of the department (Lang, 2005). Unlike his colleagues, Lang appreciated what the candidate would bring to the department rather than if he or she would uphold the status quo.

For the search committee, the task becomes an opportunity for collegial reflection so as to determine in what direction faculty wants the department to proceed given an opportunity to hire a new faculty member. Having to replace five people in one search may indicate to a candidate the degree to which that department may be experiencing dysfunction. Department turnover resulting from faculty accepting positions elsewhere denotes potential problems. Not selecting the best candidate but rather filling the position with a person willing to accept the offer may mean the committee will be searching again soon (Cohen, 2004).

Asking an untenured, inexperienced person to chair the committee further indicates a potential problem (Landrum & Clump, 2004). Appointing an inexperienced search committee chair for a mammoth task like this places the candidates at a disadvantage politically because the chair's knowledge of the department cannot be as comprehensive as it needs to be. Recognizing that a department may be dysfunctional, should the department chair/dean bring five new people into a dysfunctional environment? How do you spin the department so it seems functional when evidence indicates otherwise? Is it fair to the prospective faculty to enter a department if it has no plan to readjust or establish functionality before or shortly after they get there? Does the dean or chair realize there are problems in the first place and what plan do these administrators have to address these issues?

The culture of the faculty and the organizational climate shape the department and college establishing levels of integrity, functionality, ethics, civility, inclusion, and tolerance (Reybold, 2008). Absent these factors, then, the department and the search committee are permitted to act in ways that could misrepresent the department even when faculty believe they are doing the right thing. Dysfunction seems to become normative after a period of time, thus, it may be difficult for incumbents to recognize the problems during their short campus visit.

Furthermore, department chairs and faculty mentors should control the service commitment for new faculty members. Junior faculty eagerness to immerse themselves in university or professional service needs to be balanced with teaching and research expectations necessary for tenure and promotion. While service participation does provide junior faculty with insight into the organizational structure and collegial culture, too much too soon could be detrimental to their success on the tenure track (Filetti, 2009; Lang, 2005). Filetti advocated that chairs or deans visibly chart junior faculty time obligations associated with service opportunities to determine maximum involvement and then impose limitations. In the vignette, Tom deliberately attempted to involve Nancy in service activities, providing her with insufficient information he knew would lure her away from her primary duties as teacher and researcher.

If asked to participate in activities that seem to be better suited to more senior level faculty, junior faculty need to bow out in their own best interest. Consulting with a trusted colleague or mentor on or off campus may be necessary to get a second opinion as situations differ. Making any decision of this nature in counsel or concert with others is strongly recommended. Women and minorities entering predominantly male-dominated professions often feel in danger and perhaps they really are because of the traditions they must overcome to simply survive (Dzeich & Weiner, 1990). Accepting positions that pull new faculty away from their duties should be avoided.

Noting that untenured professors feel apprehensive about speaking up on key matters that involve them, but also haunt them down the road, calls for intervention. Not since the provost contacted untenured professors in the earlier vignette have there been similar instances of which I am aware. The dean recognized the situation of silent untenured professors and contacted the provost to discuss the dilemma. The provost who called the untenured faculty should be commended. While some faculty and administrators may think the provost overstepped his bounds, he, at the very least, showed the junior faculty whom he called that he cared about *their* future. He demonstrated that he cared in which direction each chair appointment may take the department and how that may affect them in the long term. Perhaps the situation would have turned out the same no matter if the provost made the calls or not, but taking the time from a very busy schedule to do so speaks volumes.

Each candidate who interviews must determine the culture of the department, especially the psychosocial health of the department and its ultimate degree of function or dysfunction (Herreid & Full, 2010; Landrum & Clump, 2004). While this may seem impossible to do during a 36-hour visit, it *is* possible to detect nuances and dysfunctions. For the candidate, deciphering the culture becomes a possible deciding point to take an offer if one is extended.

Search committees often ask candidates why they are seeking the position for which they applied. Perhaps someone expressing total honesty may say, "Because I hate where I work now and I want out." I have never encountered that person. Rather, we expect candidates to say that they want more challenges, or that they feel that this program is on the move and they want to be a part of it, or some other engaging response. Of course, we may silently question the sincerity of that response but, then again, we may be totally aghast at the former response. Using an interview and subsequent job offer to get your institution to increase your salary or benefits probably is more common that we would like to believe but no less tacky, if not unethical, given limited departmental resources for candidate interviews. Insincerity and deception on any level, for any reason, by either party, creates a falseness that ultimately makes it difficult to determine departmental fit. Again, we use and expect façades but not insincerity and deception.

In the earlier vignette when the dean told the faculty that a minority candidate would open up another line faculty position, he skewed and tainted the whole search process. The goal became to hire the candidate no matter what because of the promise that particular hiring entailed. Faculty could not objectively or effectively weigh all the new information and simultaneously listen to one voice of opposition. A quest for the dangling carrot unfortunately meant high stakes poker and, in this instance, the players stood to lose everything.

Undoubtedly, the best outcome of a job search is for the top candidate to do well enough for the university to extend an offer and then for the candidate to accept it. Of course, the worst is performing well but still receiving the rejection letter. The question of 'What went wrong?' lingers with the candidate. Having the ability to experience closure, knowing what went wrong, or what circumstances caused the committee to not extend an offer helps ease the pain (Reybold, 2008). Carefully screening and vetting top candidates should be a primary task. Search committee chairs rarely receive release time to fulfill their duties. These vignettes illustrate the need to consider that option, especially if it involves hiring multiple candidates from one committee.

Not every search committee is as vigilant as it needs to be given time constraints. It takes time and patience to vet candidates. Applications are laden with reference letters from the best the candidate can muster. Calling those listed becomes an arduous task. To counterbalance that, search committees, unfortunately, have been known to contact non-listed colleagues, in confidence, to seek information that would not likely be contained in any reference letter. Personally, I have received emails and phone calls from search committee members asking about former colleagues who seek employment at their institution. The uncertainty of search committee decisions causes members to gather information from those colleagues more experienced with the candidate but for which the candidate did not authorize the giving of a reference. Should you follow the old rule: "If you can't say something nice, don't say anything at all"? Not saying anything at all tends to tell the more incriminating tale regardless of your intentions. Best to respond with, "Unless the candidate knows you are calling me, in all good conscience, I cannot respond." Because so much is as stake, we understand why search committees choose this route and keep it quiet but faculty place themselves in a potential quagmire for approaching the process this way.

Failed faculty searches or reopened searches affect future searches in terms of attracting new candidates. Failed searches also contribute to lowered faculty morale. One reason for the failure may be the search committee approach of "courting the candidate." Courting candidates may be less effective than applying known faculty skills of research, inquiry, or scholarship. Cohen (2004) suggested focusing on sifting through candidate applications looking for evidence of maturity of performance. This needs to be juxtaposed with the department missions and goals. Phone and on-campus interviews may be more revealing and productive if the faculty questions reached more in-depth levels than a preponderance of basic, superficial, or typical questions. Many of the latter type questions tend to be repeated as the candidate's interview progresses. When the faculty meets to vote on the candidate, the dialog yields insufficient data with which to make an informed decision. Carl's peers may have benefited from this process as more in-depth inquiry may have yielded them an impression of George similar to his.

The theme that threaded through these vignettes illustrated a collegial "culture of silence" (Harris & Hartley, 2011). Junior faculty appear apprehensive about speaking up in front of senior colleagues. Search committees present candidates' files to faculty who seem cavalier about the process and take information at face value. When one faculty member spoke honestly against a candidate, the faculty failed to listen (culture of deafness).

Discovering a good fit between department and candidate illustrates the collegial process in action. To not take it seriously by a cavalier vote, drumming fingers on the table during a presentation, or offering a calm silence during meetings diminishes the collegium. Poskanzer (2002) summarized the ramifications aptly when he said, "Cavalier disregard of faculty opinions on matters with academic ramifications can damage morale and the healthy functioning of the institution" (p. 107). Segments of these vignettes illustrate these outcomes.

Perhaps we need to take the interview process more seriously. Perhaps search committee work must be given more importance than it currently receives in order for faculty to avoid costly short cuts. Search committees may need to be accountable for their work to ensure they do it thoroughly. Perhaps the interview process should also be taken more seriously by candidates, especially when hiring internal ones.

The search process offers no guarantees for the candidates who long for the dean's or chair's call extending a job offer. Others wait for a rejection letter that at least brings them closure. The search committee waits for recognition that typically never comes. New faculty wait to see if they made the correct decision to accept the offer as do faculty who desire to know if they made the best choice when extending it. Altering the process through deception, dangling carrots, dishonesty, or silence, negates it such that the faculty will likely have to repeat the process in a few years. Faculty need to socialize and nurture current and future members of the collegium toward ethical behavior in the search process (Reybold, 2008). Placing faculty on search committees tends to be yet another feature of the collegial role that could use a bit of faculty development to ensure the integrity of the process.

While I have probably just scratched the surface of academic search committees, you should have some idea that this process is laden with ethical issues as numerous as the number of characters involved. You have peeked into the culture of academe as some of the veil begins to be lifted. As each aspect of the faculty role is addressed, more of that mystique will be chiseled away. But before we leave I want to bring closure to the vignettes and tell you what happened to the main characters.

THE REST OF THE STORY

Nancy maintained her distance from Tom because she had lost trust in him. Fortunately, by Nancy's tenure time, Tom no longer served as chair. George remained at his old institution and eventually received tenure there. As a result, Carl's program lost their line faculty position because no other candidate accepted an offer. Norm served as department head for several years where he continued to publish prolifically in scholarly journals. In three years, Liz retired and received a monthly pension check somewhat less than she had hoped. Eventually, Bill got his wish and became department head when Norm stepped down. Russell retired several years after his unsuccessful bid for department head. After serving as department head, Scott moved up the ladder to well-respected associate dean and eventually became a dean at another university. Harry took a position at a more prestigious university near a major eastern US city. We do not know if Harry falsified his credentials to secure the new position.

BEST PRACTICES

- Regard search committee work as an honor, not another task that overextends faculty, especially novice faculty. New faculty have disciplinary expertise to offer search committees but tenured faculty should be installed as chair.

- Junior faculty should chart their service in departments so that as untenured or non-tenure track faculty members they are not placed in precarious positions that overextend them or find them in potentially politically charged circumstances (Koblinsky, Kuvalanka, & McClintock-Comeaux, 2006).

- Candidates and committees should take the screening and vetting process seriously by being as thorough as possible and by remembering to protect the propriety, integrity, and confidentiality of the process. The interview process should place faculty in the role of promoters of their department and programs. Consider the interview a collegial privilege, not a cause to leverage one's current circumstance.

- Junior faculty members may need to express their sentiments about candidates to respected senior colleagues or administrators if they feel airing their concerns in public places them in a precarious situation.

RESOURCES

- Faculty should check with their dean and/or Human Resources department to locate their institution's faculty search committee guidelines manual. It is probably accessible online. An online search will turn up manuals from other institutions that can provide additional information as to how other campuses handle the process.

- The *Inside Higher Education* website provides readers with topical commentary on various issues, including faculty searches, at www.insidehighered.com/advice.

- The Association for the Study of Higher Education (ASHE) meets annually for faculty who teach in graduate higher education administration departments. At their 2012 conference they conducted a free early career faculty workshop. Other large associations that do not already offer such mentoring opportunities may consider contacting ASHE for information at www.ashe.ws to learn more.

Chapter 3

Classroom Teaching and Evaluation

INTRODUCTION

Hundreds of books and scholarly articles have been published on how to teach college students (see Wilbert McKeachie). Manuals exist to help faculty write syllabi, formulate test questions, create grading rubrics, lecture effectively, and conduct lively class discussions. Newer texts guide faculty through cooperative learning, computer-assisted instruction, simulations, online applications, and automated computer-assisted design. Campus faculty development seminars abound for instructors wishing to improve face-to-face and online teaching skills, understand new cohorts of students, and translate course material into effective evaluation tools. Some campuses offer peer-assessed, mid-semester, formative evaluations to assist faculty with improving instruction.

Unfortunately, there are important topics that faculty seldom broach. For instance, rarely do faculty sit and discuss the results of their end-of-semester evaluations with anyone other than their department chairs/heads at their annual performance evaluation. Unique and highly personal evaluations of teaching tend to fall into the same category as love letters (minus the love). Although faculty may complain in the aggregate about student quality, they tend not to reveal individual classroom disruptions, poor performance on most student exams or papers, or student hostilities toward them personally and probably to their detriment.

Faculty rarely engage one another in conversations about the greatest act of student disrespect toward them: plagiarism, stealing someone else's work and passing it off as their own. Academic dishonesty places a professor in a very precarious position. Overlooking the act does a disservice to the rest of the class who honestly complete assignments. Pursuing a case against the student takes time and investigative skill; for example, locating university policy on academic honesty and following it explicitly or taking the student before the academic honesty committee. Even though faculty tend to maintain their silence, the following vignettes indicate reasons why keeping silent should trouble us all.

Student Evaluations of Faculty Teaching

Susie realized that evaluations could indeed provide important information if students approached them from a thoughtful perspective. She knew that some students, who perceived that they would not get the high grade they wanted, may use the evaluation as a means to trash her. Thus far, her evaluations for the tougher courses had been lower than courses for which students had an affinity and tended to rate her higher.

During one semester, Susie's introductory graduate class for some reason did not proceed as well as she had hoped or as similar classes had in the past. This may have been an unusual group of students. Perhaps her frame of mind as a result of some minor medical issues could have tempered her disposition in a less than positive way. Whatever the reason, maybe the student responses would give her some insight.

When the evaluations arrived, Susie realized the overall score was slightly lower than it had been for that course previously. But, she remained optimistic and satisfied, given the circumstances of the semester. As she began to read the written comments, they were better than she had expected, that is until she reached the last one. That student wrote, "It doesn't matter if you have tenure, lady, there are other ways to get rid of you."

Shaken, Susie read it again, trying to figure out who may have written that statement and why. She did not recognize the handwriting. It would be pointless to speculate anyway, she thought. Instead, she showed it to her department chair. Susie insisted it was a threat and should be handled as such. The chair interpreted it differently and told her it was probably nothing.

Each college/university offers a standard multiple choice evaluation form with space for students to write comments. Departments provide faculty with an average class score and a typed list of student comments in the days following the close of the semester. These scores and comments are private assessments intended for the professor and the chair to discuss during the yearly performance evaluation. Susie approached her chair, shaken and demeaned by the comments she read. He dismissed her concern as trivial. To Susie, it was not trivial. Her concern had little to do with her tenure and promotion but rather her safety. The least the chair could have done was speak with her and probe with her any concerns she had during her class to attempt to help her get to the root cause of the comment and at the very least settle her concerns. She shared her experience with a close colleague who appeared as dumbfounded at Susie by the comment and the chair's response.

Students probably operate under the assumption that their written comments on the scan sheet will be typed and the trail back to them through handwriting analysis will be stopped. Susie possessed the original forms. The fact that Susie may be able to identify this irate student through handwriting, on the one hand, may have helped Susie figure out who disliked her. With minimal detective work, the culprit could have been identified. On the other hand, the implied standard of care that permitted the student to express himself or herself confidentially appeared to be breached. This is not to excuse the student as the comments on the form are conceived in the spirit of assisting faculty in improving teaching practices, not scaring them. Susie expected to hear constructive comments from students, but when she saw this, it demeaned the evaluation process as a legitimate means to obtain information on teacher performance.

Why Semesters Should be Shorter

As we all know semesters are 15 to 16 weeks long and terms are 10 weeks. We have two semesters and three terms during a regular academic year. Having been a professor in both environments, Jill realized that each format had its perks and drawbacks. When she taught courses for which she and her students had a deep affinity and genuine interest, the longer the better. However, class composition can enhance or shatter that dream. Jill's class from hell included three personality types that contrasted with the other nine people in the class so much so that she dreaded each night during the 15 weeks it was offered. She guessed it was the same for those nine people who also had to endure the same experience.

One student, Matt, utilized his laptop for most of the class, periodically spouting caustic comments to his classmates and Jill. She presumed that because no one else was taking notes but listening attentively and engaging in the discussion that Matt elected to use his laptop for personal reasons. She emailed the class following the second night to inform them that using laptops interfered with the class and would no longer be permitted. Matt promptly informed her that she singled him out and that he was taking notes and he should be permitted to use his laptop. Another student who sat next to Matt in class confirmed her suspicions. He told Jill that Matt was on the computer surfing the Internet, answering emails, or completing tasks from his day job.

When Jill returned graded papers to students after midterms, another student, Lee, challenged his grade. She explained in detail to him after class the reason why he had earned a lower than expected grade. Lee told her that he deserved better. Jill explained that she had standards for students such that they must perform at the graduate level in order to secure a high grade and Lee had not performed at that level. Lee informed Jill that he was a gay, disabled veteran, and thus untouchable.

While these two instances were one-time things, each week the presence of another student in class skewed the participation dynamic. During three of the 15 weeks Frank was absent, the class discussions proved engaging, of high quality, and inclusive of all members. The other 12 weeks Frank not only tried to monopolize the night's discussion but gave the impression that only he had the proper interpretation of the material. From his vantage point at his new job on campus, Frank felt that he truly informed his classmates more than the instructor, because, as he implied, she did not work in an administrative capacity, as he did. Needless to say that semester was a long 15 weeks!

Entitlement crept into the faculty vocabulary more than a decade ago. Newer generations of students, thought of as consumers of higher education, demand more for the high tuition they are paying. While the tuition only buys students a seat in the classroom, they tend to extrapolate more from the pricy transaction: a higher grade; freedom to disrupt the class or conduct their personal business; occasion to monopolize the classroom discussion; and take opportunities to disrespect professors and fellow classmates.

Classrooms become self-contained physical and emotional spaces. Typically discussions from classes remain confidential. If not taped, the discussion flows only from memory and not from a transcribed script. More importantly, these spaces bounded by four walls enclose emotions as well. Although Jill regarded this class as one of her worst, she discussed it with no one, not her peers, closest colleagues, or the department chair. Perhaps faculty development may have been helpful during this semester in the form of a mid-semester peer review but none was requested. She did not schedule an appointment with the faculty development office even though she knew it existed to assist her. Jill trudged along alone dreading each class except the three classes Frank missed.

Surely Jill's demeanor could be read by the other class members because they too experienced the same dynamic. Because the class dynamic changed in Frank's absence, she knew his presence in the class affected them as much as it did her. None of them scheduled an appointment with Jill to talk about their frustrations. No one in the class took it upon themselves to approach Frank, publically in class or in private outside of class. Perhaps the students waited for Jill. She seemed to have no trouble instituting the no laptop policy and evaluating Lee accurately and holding steadfast. But they could see she was not able to neutralize Frank.

Beware, the Dean and I are Buddies

When Leah returned in January refreshed from her fall sabbatical, she greeted a new student in her program who looked to be about the same age as she. Leah showed surprise when the student introduced himself as Duane, struck up a conversation, and called her by her first name rather than professor or doctor as was standard procedure across the department. Duane made a point to mention that he had worked closely with the dean on several projects during the fall and that is why he sought admission to this program. Leah learned that Duane would be in one of her classes this semester.

During that first class, as everyone made their introduction, Leah realized that other students in class referred to her formally so she anticipated that Duane would take the hint and follow protocol. He persisted upon calling all faculty members and administrators by their first names, including the dean. Eventually, Leah pulled him aside and suggested that out of respect for the faculty, he address them more formally. Very apologetic, Duane agreed.

At semester's end, Duane presented his paper in class and handed it into Leah. She regarded the presentation as substandard, despite the fact that Duane came across as pretentious and haughty during class. Leah read his paper and concluded it barely met the expectations for graduate level work. His participation throughout the semester rated average in that he engaged in frequent banter often devoid of scholarly content. She concluded that his work earned him no more than a C or C+. This would not help his standing with the admissions committee.

When Duane received his grade, he phoned Leah to yell at her for rating his work so shabbily. Before he rudely hung up on her, Duane announced that he would report her to the dean. The next day Leah received a call from her chair who had received a call from the dean. Her chair asked her to resolve the issue.

If the professor wants to understand his or her students, he or she must enter the student world in order to perceive faculty from the student perspective. Ask Rebekah Nathan (2005), anthropologist and author of *My Freshman Year*. Her insights proved valuable to subsequent classroom instruction and course development. By the same token, graduate students need initially to separate the role of student from that of budding professional (Weidman, Twale, & Stein, 2001). Because of his personal and professional association with the dean, Duane presumed an elevated status for himself that was incongruent with the role of student in the classroom. He embellished that relationship with the dean to parlay his way through Leah's class, the admissions process, and the program. Duane expected that relationship to open doors and influence people. From the information provided, Leah found it difficult to determine if his relationship with the dean was as Duane interpreted and acted upon.

Duane's disrespect for Leah, although less significant at first, escalated considerably when he realized she regarded his work as below graduate level. His response of challenging her evaluation skills, yelling at her, and hanging up the phone indicated as much about his role as graduate student as it did as budding professional (Weidman et al., 2001). The program goal of turning out leaders in the professional field well versed in communication, problem-solving, and decision-making skills eluded Duane as well. He clearly demonstrated on several levels that he may not be a good candidate for the program.

Leah did not report this information to her chair. She probably felt no need to report it. It did not surprise her that Duane asked the dean for help. Nor did the dean's complacency on the issue surprise her, even though he went through normal channels to convey his message. We have no way of knowing the conversation between Duane and the dean nor the dean's take on the matter. Duane probably did not indicate his disrespectful behavior toward Leah during their meeting. But, clearly, the dean could have stopped the conversation and told Duane that he respected Leah's ability to judge graduate level work. Accept the C+ and be thankful. But he passed the matter off onto his underling, the chair, who responded in kind.

Duane, feeling that he was entitled to a better grade, flexed his muscle with the dean in order to hopefully get it. Again, we do not know the real relationship between the two, only Duane's perceptions and interpretation. Based on the evidence, either the dean avoided confrontation with Duane and passed the matter down the line, or they *were* in fact good buddies and thus he supported Duane's cause. However, the dean and chair's response only served to circumvent faculty autonomy.

In the final analysis, Duane was permitted to win the battle *and* the war. The dean should have stood by Leah and closed the case immediately without ever involving her but instead he chose to pass the matter along to her department chair. Forcing the chair to do his bidding only indicated the dean's blatant disregard for Leah, the chair, Duane's fellow students, faculty autonomy, and graduate program standards.

How Many Times Can You Violate Academic Honesty Codes?

In her graduate class, Margaret enjoyed the interaction of her students save one, Judy. Typically the entrance of Judy in the class made the other students cringe. After several courses with Judy, students realized that her drinking problem affected not only her classroom performance but theirs as well. Her slurred words, hostile attitude toward classmates and Margaret, and her inability to respond accurately to questions Margaret posed, made for a long class.

As the term happily drew to a close, students handed in their term papers. When Margaret proceeded through the pile to Judy's paper, she read with interest as well as confusion. The paper read too perfectly, not the typical master's level paper but instead one that mirrored something Margaret thought had already been published. (In the days before software was designed to easily discover errant student work, faculty had to uncover plagiarism by hand.) Margaret began with the reference list and located several of the books listed there. She headed for the library the next day. Sadly, she confirmed her suspicions. Judy had not only extracted pages of text from one book, she also stole the section headings, making it much easier for Margaret to find.

Because Judy came from another program, Margaret made an appointment with Judy's advisor to discuss what she had found. Don perused the paper and informed Margaret that it was the same paper that Judy had turned in for his class last semester. With egg on his face, Don admitted that he had no idea it was plagiarized. According to the student handbook, Judy violated another rule by handing in the same paper in two courses. Margaret also informed the chair of Judy's department and the chair of her own department. Because of the unstable nature of Judy's behavior, Margaret remained concerned for her own safety.

CLASSROOM TEACHING AND EVALUATION

As per the academic honesty policy, Margaret awarded Judy an Incomplete grade. Incensed, Judy filed a grievance against Margaret. Margaret received the papers from the grievance committee during the time frame that she filed papers to the academic honesty committee against Judy. Margaret called the chair of the grievance committee to inform her of what was transpiring and the chair agreed to hold off until the academic honesty committee determined the outcome of the plagiarism issues.

When the academic honesty committee hearing approached, Judy attended and appeared intoxicated. She argued with the committee members and threatened Margaret. She denied that she had plagiarized any material from the book in question. Margaret went to great pains to highlight the plagiarized work in Judy's paper and, then, align it with the pages in the book from which Judy copied. Margaret left no doubt with the academic honesty committee that Judy had violated not only that policy but with Don's acknowledgment handed the paper in twice.

Margaret experienced a similar problem as Jill, a disruptive student in her class. While Jill managed to address some of her issues, she could not address them all. Clearly, professorial training in graduate school covers little to nothing about pedagogy or andragogy. Jill and Margaret and their colleagues muddle through, often using trial and error. But Judy posed an additional problem about which faculty know little. Although Judy created disruptions and skewed the dynamic of class, her alcoholism raised additional concerns of safety.

Over time students in Margaret's class from Judy's department informed Margaret of Judy's classroom behavior and her drinking bouts. Surely Judy's advisor knew of the issues as did some of the faculty in that department. No one afforded Margaret a head's up or, worse yet, did anything to assist Judy with her problems. They enabled her. This is ironic, as Judy's degree program was counseling. Not resolving this issue may have led to Judy's ability to get away with her academic dishonesty. Ironic that the faculty in the department enabled her there was well.

Faculty dread finding what Margaret discovered, that is, a plagiarized paper. They abhor plagiarism even more when they learn this is not the first time, and that that plagiarized paper was submitted twice. Because the paper appeared to be too professional for a graduate student to write, and given prior faculty knowledge of Judy's alcoholic rants, a quick check by her professors to determine if Judy's work was original should have been forthcoming. But, that was not the case. There is no way to ever determine if other material Judy submitted proved to be her original work. Faculty never looked. Again, there is no way to determine if these professors were not reading the papers carefully, were concerned for their own safety, or were told by someone in authority to just press onward.

Enter Margaret, who knew nothing initially about Judy or her situation. Margaret could have looked the other way, too. Margaret could have gone to the department chair earlier in the semester when Judy made class disruption a habit.

She did not examine policy or even check to see if a campus policy on alcohol abuse existed or covered students. She thought she could handle the situation. Again students in the classroom like those in Jill's class did nothing except inform Margaret of the long-standing problem. No one wanted to take on Judy, only enable her through their silence or inactivity.

Margaret could not deal with the obvious dishonesty issue and risked her reputation taking Judy to committee. Judy's retaliation made Margaret wonder if it was all worth it. Margaret's conversation with the chair of the grievance committee appeared to be the only support she received in the whole ordeal. She received minimal support from Judy's department or her own. Margaret's action brought previous faculty silence and complacency to light. Even though that department should have come to Margaret's rescue in a major show of support, they sent her out on a limb with a chainsaw still not wanting to deal with Judy and the problems her drinking caused for them, the students, and Margaret. Margaret took the time to present an airtight case against Judy, something no one in Judy's department cared to do. Getting Judy out of the program, either through Judy dropping out on her own or graduating, seemed to be their strategy. With Judy's issues, her counseling department should have shown more concern and compassion but sadly they did not.

DEBRIEFING CLASSROOM TEACHING AND EVALUATION

Teacher evaluations are emotional experiences for students in that they evoke positive *and* negative feelings about the material, the instructor, the assignments, the tests, and the grade. Often the results of the instruments used to assess faculty effectiveness actually measure student perception more than reality (Beyers, 2008). Student evaluation results tend to be based on how the student enjoyed the class, which renders the score unreliable (Kekes, 1996). Student evaluations may have their place in academe but students may not be able to evaluate what administrators expect them to evaluate. Instead the practice supports how we value consumerism and customer satisfaction.

Professors use their professional judgment when evaluating student performance in a course and, then, award the grade the student earns. Faculty must be able to defend their assessment of students based on a rubric, a scale, or some other uniformly used measurement tool (Poskanzer, 2002). On evaluations, we assume that students evaluate objectively, too. In other words, students must separate their like or dislike for the subject matter from the professor delivering it. Sometimes one aspect bleeds into the other, however, and distracts students from an honest and true teacher evaluation. Students in their evaluating cannot be expected to reach that same standard of care used by faculty. However, the evaluating administrator often presumes they do. The results of student evaluations affect faculty career advancement through the tenure process. As a result, the evaluation process at some institutions has evolved into a popularity contest. When students learn that a faculty member gives all As, the classroom seats may fill up quickly. By contrast, students can disrespect faculty by ranting and raving on the written part of the evaluation form as did Susie's graduate student.

Perhaps because evaluations are mandatory, the collegial culture rejects what the managerial culture imposes (Bergquist & Pawlak, 2008). Because students rather than peers render these decisions, faculty may dismiss evaluations as ignoble. Whatever the reason or bias, student evaluations of faculty teaching uniformly given are not uniformly esteemed (Bjorklund & Rehling, 2010). Some faculty read the results and make alternations to their courses because they view the process as formative. When the class evaluation information becomes available weeks after the course ends, the formative nature of the assessment tends to be lost, however. Lang (2005) reasoned that his evaluations occurring after the close of the semester seemed more summative than formative. Administrators and tenure committees tend to see the information as summative even if it is intended otherwise.

One student in Susie's class expressed his or her emotions regarding his or her perception of Susie. Student emotions triggered an emotional response in Susie, as well. Eiszler (2002) posited that administrators over-interpret these evaluations, perhaps lending too much credence to the information students provide. In Susie's case, her chair placed little credence in the emotionally laden, written comment. It would be interesting to know why he dismissed the interpretation of the comment as threatening, and in contrast, how much he valued the quantitative scores as a measure of teacher effectiveness in his evaluations of Susie's classroom performance when he assessed merit pay.

Fisanick (2006) noted how teacher evaluations have "the potential power to undermine a teacher's success" (p. 332) and raise the degree of student power, authority and consumerism on campus (Stark-Wroblewski, Ahlering, & Brill, 2007). Students may hold the evaluation as a means to control the situation in their favor (Ross, 1910). Through their research, Pan, Tan, Ragupathi, Booluck, Roop, and Ip (2009) cannot be certain what motivations students use to evaluate faculty and how students arrive at their responses. Students may base their responses on perceptions of learning or of the instructor personally as in Susie's case. Because student cohorts feel more empowered, seek immediacy, harbor inflated expectations, and take a casual attitude toward their studies, faculty like Susie cannot always use the information to assist them in pedagogical improvement or even regard it as valid (Lippman, Bulanda, & Wagenaar, 2009).

Reliance on quantifiable statistics to measure teaching coupled with the students' presence in the classroom to willingly respond satisfies a rationale for administrative use of the results (Cahn, 1994) regardless of their validity (Stark-Wroblewski et al., 2007). Thus, we evaluate to fulfill merit pay and tenure and promotion requirements rather than to have an affect on a professor's teaching while it is taking place and in need of immediate response. In other words, administrators have elevated evaluations from a formative to summative status (Crumbly, Flinn, & Reichelt, 2010). Jill could have used an intervention midway through her class. Able to handle some minor situations, she felt inadequate and ineffective at handling major ones. Speaking to her department chair and/or contacting her faculty development office should have been options. Faculty development office staff appears all too eager to assist faculty. To do so, however, requires that Jill admit she has a problem for which she cannot find the solution. Encouragement from administration and faculty development to utilize their services without prejudice should be the priority of academic administrators.

Faculty relationships with and obligations to graduate students differ from undergraduates but the evaluation forms tend to be identical. Faculty also assess the graduate student's socialization into the role and as future members of their profession (Weidman et al., 2001). Faculty has to evaluate students objectively on their papers, exams, projects, and participation, but we also hold graduate students to a professional standard as well that goes beyond scores on papers, projects, and tests. Perhaps Jill could have stated her philosophy of education and her graduate level expectations of her students in the initial class meeting and in the syllabus as a way to socialize them as students as well as begin to socialize future professionals to the normative standards of practice and behavior in her professional area (Bjorklund & Rehling, 2010; Bray & Del Favero, 2004; Lippman et al., 2009; Weidman et al., 2001). Given the changes in successive cohorts of students entering the academy, institutions will need to address through faculty development how faculty can update their pedagogical techniques to reach effectively future student cohorts (Lippman et al., 2009).

To regard the student as consumer drives how faculty and administrators may use evaluations (Eiszler, 2002) and causes the student to see the evaluations in a different capacity than either group intended. Furthermore, Slaughter (2001) contended, "when universities think of students as consumers, they *package* themselves to entice students" and, as a result, "students no longer see themselves as apprentices who come to the university to sit at the feet of distinguished scholars and enjoy learning for its own sake" (p. 25). Faculty may be conducting classes to appease students rather than teaching to the truth of the discipline when the results of evaluations stand to affect negatively their tenure, promotion, and/or merit pay (Hora, 2012; Thompson, 2006).

Jill treaded lightly around Lee, Frank, and Matt. Margaret treaded lightly around Judy. In all cases, student incivility toward Jill and Margaret affected the classroom learning climate. Not only were Jill and Margaret affected, but Bjorklund and Rehling (2010) concluded in their study that students appear to be cognizant of classmate disruptive behaviors as well. In fact, these researchers found that "students perceive a fair amount of moderately uncivil behavior in their classes on a regular basis" (p. 17). The students in the study regarded the most uncivil behaviors as continuing to talk when asked to stop and attending class under the influence of drugs or alcohol. Hirschy and Braxton (2004) focused on the deleterious effects that ignoring these disruptions have on students in the class. Students can fail to engage in the class, feel isolated, and/or drop the class. If faculty and students share in the teaching and learning process, each group has a mutual stake in arresting incivilities such as Judy and Frank's classroom disruptions.

With an increased sense of entitlement, students feel that they deserve more for less effort and expect better treatment despite their behavior. These students projected an 'inflated self-esteem.' Leah encountered this from Duane and his self-elevated stance as a result of being friends with her dean. Jill witnessed this entitlement through a student's overreliance on virtual communication, another's just-in-time/just-for-me expectations, and from all three, a decreased status distinction between student and faculty (Greenberger, Lessard, Chen, & Farruggia, 2008). None of their behaviors contribute to the learning process or their professional socialization into their field (Weidman et al., 2001).

However, Lampman, Phelps, Bancroft, and Beneke (2009), in their study of contrapower harassment, report that 96–99 percent of faculty, regardless of gender, reported frequent levels of classroom disruption. Yelling was reported by 29 percent of faculty respondents and 'threatening' communications by 24 percent. Hirschy and Braxton (2004) summarized that almost all faculty experience classroom disruptive behaviors and incivilities but fail to report, confront, or discuss them, preferring to deal with their own frustrations in isolation. Heike, Hazen, and Theobold (2010) learned from their study that while behaviors were not always hostile, almost every participant in the study reported dealing with some uncivil student behavior.

Although men in the Lampman et al. (2009) study reported more instances of hostility in their classes than women, female faculty regarded these disruptive behaviors as more distressing or upsetting to them than did their male colleagues. Women who sought support, however, experienced more negative responses than men. Because Margaret had tenure, she probably felt more secure taking Judy to committee but then again her counseling colleagues also had tenure but did not cross Judy. Judy filed a grievance against Margaret. Would she have done the same to her male professors? While men in this study experienced slightly more incivility, the study did not cover the intensity of contrapower instances as predicted by gender. However, because they found that women are more likely than men to seek action against contrapower harassment behaviors, women may indicate a higher level of severity and/or distress caused by the student.

Taken individually or together, these negative entitlement behaviors affect class dynamics and outcomes (Westerman, Bergman, Bergman, & Daly, 2012). Boice (1996) determined that because faculty resist revealing problems that occur in their classrooms, classroom incivilities are seldom discussed with colleagues.

In fact, Crumbly et al. (2010) contended that some professors overlook negative student behaviors and deliberately pander to students to obtain higher evaluations. These practices cause students to overestimate their own knowledge and performance levels and may contribute to their elevating their status in relationship to the professor. Duane serves as a perfect example by using his connection with the dean to leverage his status and eventually his grade. In all vignettes, some student disrupters or harassers received little or no initial reprimand from faculty.

Inconsistency among faculty grading practices allows students to assume that similar amounts of effort in all classes will be consistently rewarded (Cahn, 1994; Eiszler, 2002). Similarly, inconsistencies in classroom policies offer the potential to confuse students about what they can and cannot do in face-to-face classes. Jill encountered that with Lee, Margaret with Judy, and Leah with Duane. Other faculty may ignore Matt and his constant use of the laptop in class but Jill stood firm on that issue. If faculty does not address such issues as a department or college and, eventually, come to some consensus, students will encounter inconsistencies and incongruence from course to course. Otherwise, students will consider themselves deserving of amenities that tend to be more disruptive to their education than helpful. Administrations need to address pandering as it relates to faculty attempting to skew favorably their course evaluations (Westerman et al., 2012).

The culture of silence gleaned from these examples reached a chilling climax in the last vignette on academic dishonesty. Faculty rarely talk about academic dishonesty, the policy that governs it, or recount instances that happen to them personally. In addition, confidentiality prevents professors from saying too much about specific cases. Faculty having to approach the student with the evidence is an emotional ordeal. However, academic dishonesty should be one area where faculty voice concern to one another. The research literature speaks to the rise of student entitlement and incivility as perhaps a cause and effect of our collective silence (Bjorklund & Rehling, 2010; Lampman et al., 2009; Lippman et al., 2009). Professors will encounter academic dishonesty at some point or in some form during their career and ignoring it should not be an option (Levy & Rakovski, 2006).

Academic honesty policies should be written to maintain standards of academic and professional performance but no two campus policies and procedures may be exactly alike. Institutions respond to the academic dishonesty issues differently even though it affects academe universally. Policy and procedures for addressing plagiarism could range from an extremely detailed university committee process, to having the dean's office assist the faculty in adjudicating the case, to letting the professor handle the situation as he or she sees fit. Some campuses uphold stringent academic honesty policies with defined sanctions, some simply have honor codes that students are expected to uphold, and others have options to fit specific situations. In the latter instance, administrators may ask faculty to reconsider a student's final grade or have the student rewrite the plagiarized sections of the paper.

Worthen (2004) asserted that "plagiarism creates the potential for deception, and deception, whether deliberate or inadvertent, cannot be countenanced in the practice of law" (p. 444). Therefore, he believed that the discipline for plagiarism should be rendered by the professor who was deceived by the student. Regardless of the adjudication process, any policy without teeth would demean any honor code and appear to acquiesce to the student as customer (Thompson, 2006). As common as cheating and plagiarism have become, faculty should resolve these issues with consistent administrative backing (Hauptman, 2002). Due to the perceptions that she may be retaliating against Judy, Margaret selected at random a few other papers in her class to scan for plagiarism in case the committee asked. Margaret did not want to appear to be vindictive toward Judy as a result of Judy's semester-long disruptive behavior.

While truth in the academy cannot embrace academic dishonesty under any circumstance, numerous empirical studies indicate that cheating and plagiarism are more common than academics can fathom (Bennett, 2005; Hard, Conway, & Moran, 2006). These studies also estimated that more plagiarism goes undiscovered and unreported by faculty. In fact, faculty sees misconduct as uncommon because they presume acts of dishonesty tend to be more unintentional than intentional. In their rationalization, students did not really mean to plagiarize their papers. Belter and duPre (2009) affirmed that academic honesty policy may or may not separate intentional dishonesty from sloppiness or ignorance of the rules but the faculty member must make that determination before seeking further action against the student. However, that determination takes time and energy and, subsequently, causes faculty and student emotional distress. Whether Margaret's colleagues suspected Judy of plagiarizing or not, they did nothing to stop it. Because Judy proved to be so disruptive in the classroom, it would seem logical for the faculty in that department to intervene, but they did nothing. There is no way to know if any conversation among Judy's department faculty regarding her behavior ever took place before Margaret opened a can of worms. Based on the work of Boice (1996), Bray and Del Favero (2004), and Hirschy and Braxton (2004), the answer is probably no.

Once several administrators knew that Judy had intentionally rather than inadvertently plagiarized her paper, they offered Margaret no support or assistance. They knew that Margaret intended to take Judy to committee and also that Judy retaliated with filing an academic grievance against Margaret. Their response appeared to be one of relief in that, finally, *someone* had held Judy's work and behavior to task. But their silence in this matter caused Margaret emotional stress, precious time, and inconvenience (Bray & Del Favero, 2004). Thompson (2006) may agree that there is a correlation between the amount of campus plagiarism reported by faculty and the administrative support of faculty who find and report it. In other words, Margaret assumed the responsibility with little support. She added another task in an already time-constrained job and addressed bureaucratic hassles including a student grievance with little or no support beyond her diligence. Perhaps faculty would come forward and address academic dishonesty if university policy explicitly identified parameters and sanctions, offered administrative support to faculty, instructed students in honest test-taking and paper-writing practices, and mandated faculty to include statements on cheating and plagiarism in their syllabi (Bennett, 2005). Academic dishonesty, while not something faculty likes to discuss, is not an area where we should tolerate silence either.

THE REST OF THE STORY

Susie never learned who wrote the threatening comment on her evaluations. The threat never came to fruition either. However, Susie pushed the department to have the administrative assistant type all the student comments before the faculty could see them to ensure student confidentiality despite the fact that the handwriting may have helped her solve the mystery. Jill celebrated enthusiastically at the close of the semester. Lee and Frank never signed up for another course Jill taught. Matt took a few more courses from Jill but remembered to leave his laptop at home. Leah chose to not honor the chair and dean's request to work with Duane to raise his grade as much to preserve her integrity as the fact that she secured a more lucrative position at another university. In accordance with university policy, Judy received the maximum punishment from the academic honesty committee. The grievance committee subsequently dismissed the case against Margaret without a hearing.

BEST PRACTICES

- Perhaps faculty teaching graduate students would benefit from a different teaching evaluation form than the ones used for undergraduate courses. In lieu of that, faculty could augment the existing forms to include more pertinent questions.

- Formative mid-semester peer and student evaluations should be available so faculty can make alterations in their courses before semester's end.

- Faculty should consider formulating classroom policies that are universal in nature and enforced universally to protect the civility of their classroom environments.

- If faculty are not aware of online software plagiarism detection programs, they need to be. Faculty need to pressure administrators to purchase access to those programs.

- Faculty must avail themselves regularly of faculty development services on campus. Faculty need to share their classroom concerns more than they do with their colleagues and their chair as well as with faculty development staff.

RESOURCES

- If your university offers online courses, plagiarism detection options probably exist such as Safe Assignment or Turnitin. Check with your instructional design and development centers for information and instruction on how to use them in online *and* face-to-face classes.

- Online websites offer plagiarism detection services, such as The Plagiarism Checker (http://www.dustball.com/cs/plagiarism.checker/) and Plagiarism Detector (http://plagiarism-detector.com/), among others.

- Wendy Sutherland-Smith's 2008 book, *Plagiarism, the Internet, and Student Learning* offers faculty a framework to help them deal with plagiarism.

- Thousands of articles and books have been written on student evaluation of college teaching. Herbert W. Marsh established a lengthy scholarly record on the topic and, thus, his articles and those with colleagues should provide faculty with a reliable body of knowledge on the subject.

- *The Journal of Faculty Development* publishes refereed articles on a variety of faculty development issues and offers suggestions for improvement.

Chapter 4

Teaching Online

Shoot, Aim, Ready

INTRODUCTION

Whether institutions offer online courses to complement undergraduate and graduate programs or offer all online programs, impetus for those courses and programs more than likely emanated from the managerial/administrative side of the academy as opposed to the faculty side. While a few pioneering professors enthusiastically embraced online education, most probably hoped it would be another passing fad. Face-to-face instruction could not be duplicated, they reasoned, and learning surely would not take place under such impersonal circumstances. How could faculty reproduce class instruction and student interaction in a virtual environment? How would faculty preserve the integrity of their programs and their own intellectual property using online technology? How much does the faculty or administration know about instructional technology, Hyper Text Markup Language (HTML) language, and uploading course information into learning management systems?

Perhaps the greatest mistake made by administrators and the worst assumption held by faculty is that one could take a face-to-face course and transition it to online without any additional considerations. Voila! Because administrators sought to deliver more courses to more people at less cost and faculty sought to minimize the work they faced transitioning to online, neither approached the benefits of online delivery by examining what the medium has to offer in terms of enhancing instructional delivery. The possibilities for learning based on the many features of the online format matched to the course objectives should generate the best results. Simply recreating the face-to-face course online rarely reproduces the tangible classroom, hence, the result is faculty disappointment and the likelihood of limited student learning. However, utilizing the many benefits of the online format with the help and guidance of trained instructional design professionals offers more options and benefits to the online instructor than could be realized in the classroom. In the following series of vignettes the situations feature faculty

39

willing to embrace online delivery but they illustrate that without assistance, especially from competent leadership and also the support from instructional design personnel, faculty encounter difficulty.

Administrative Support—This Should Not be an Oxymoron

Diane worked for a not-for-profit online institution to help them build a new doctoral program and launch it. The dean with whom she originally spoke informed her that technical support to help her set up the course shell for the first entering cohort would be forthcoming. He assured Diane that the admissions staff would be instrumental in following up with prospective student contacts. In addition, he reassured her that the instructional design folks would assist her with ideas on how to deliver course content to ensure maximum quality.

During the semester in which Diane and her faculty team of colleagues began to design the program and their individual courses, they seemed to hit one obstacle after another. As they prepared to welcome the first cohort to campus, the admissions director regretted to inform them that they had only one paid student. Diane contacted the marketing department and asked to see the materials they distributed to prospective students. When she saw that the information in the literature exactly matched that of other doctoral programs at the institution, Diane asked the staff if she could rewrite the information to more clearly reflect the new program. The marketing staff regretted to inform her that there was no budget to print all new materials. Diane and her colleague, Joyce, asked the instructional design director if they could peek into an existing online course that he regarded as a best practices example. He regretted to inform them that he could not do that. When Diane submitted her course materials for the technical staff to upload into the online format, they regretted to inform her that the deadline for that service was the previous day and they could not help her. Diane and her colleagues appealed to their department chair for help.

One obstacle would have been understandable but four of them bordered on political maneuvering. When the team along with their department chair brainstormed about the situation, they concluded that the new program created more work for instructional support staff and perhaps may compete for students contemplating existing doctoral programs. As a result, they suspected that a coalition of individual administrators sought to halt the team's forward progress and stall the degree. Not to be defeated, the team of faculty and their chair proceeded without staff support to recruit and interview students, design courses and upload them into the web format, and design their own marketing materials. In the meantime, they and the department chair did their own detective work to determine who may be trying to sabotage their new program.

Clearly the time spent on the detective work detracted from the time they each needed to construct their courses. The department chair proved instrumental in assisting with their needs, championing their efforts, diverting funds to financially support their marketing efforts, and questioning staff discretely until she and the team pieced together the situation. Their collective efforts unearthed a multitude of administrative blunders that eventually caught the attention of the university president. As the program struggled to the launch pad, the faculty and chair formed a collegial bond forged by their efforts to unravel the mystery.

Technical Support—When You Have it and When You Don't

Sherri contracted with two institutions to teach part-time online. University A boasted state-of-the-art facilities, competent faculty, and highly capable technical support staff. The instructional design staff asked Sherri to fill in their Word document template and give it to the IT department, informing her that their IT team would transition the material to the course shell in a day's time. Faculty skilled in instructional design assisted Sherri with course arrangement, innovative ideas, and alternatives and options for delivering course content. IT staff performed troubleshooting as the course progressed. The IT staff produced aesthetic courses that upheld program quality and that appeared consistent across the college. Sherri learned volumes from working with this university's instructional faculty leader and support team and staff.

University B administration loved to hear when any faculty member wanted to teach online. Sherri asked her chair about the university's instructional design department and if they would supply her with their template. The department chair had no idea what she was talking about. The web-based format they used was unfamiliar to Sherri, so she asked for assistance with uploading the course content into the shell. Again, the department chair thought there may be a graduate assistant who possibly may be able to help her but he was not absolutely sure. Sherri met with a graduate assistant and he agreed to help, but he told her this was not his area of expertise or a top priority and it would probably take him weeks to upload her new course. Given Sherri's dearth of knowledge of their online delivery format, she appreciated his help immensely. Once Sherri acclimated to the University B system, she updated her own course content each semester. Impressed, program administrators asked Sherri how to maximize the online delivery format and increase course offerings.

Contrasting philosophies of web-based instruction separate University A from University B. Each program wished to embrace online learning, yet only one proved ready and able to deliver it properly as well as able to offer faculty support and assistance. To enter online delivery, University B does a disservice to the students and dissuades faculty from approaching online delivery with an open mind. To assume that faculty can simply transition a face-to-face class to an online format is a fallacious assumption. Online formats offer faculty the greater use of technology and to not incorporate technology to the fullest extent to enhance a course misuses the medium and renders the course more tedious for the students and faculty.

Because faculty tend to resist online delivery, University A made the transition much easier and more palatable for the instructors while University B entered the competition without a game plan. University B administration should not have encouraged online delivery until they had the resources in place to support faculty. Because of Sherri's adjunct status, she accepted the task rather than turn it down until the chair or dean had the foresight to employ staff before encouraging online delivery. Sherri felt she possessed enough information and experience to adapt her skills to University B course development in order to successfully deliver the course but not without some apprehension and frustration. However, without additional assistance forthcoming from the University B dean's office, other tenured faculty new to online delivery would be less likely to contemplate teaching online or using online hybrid models to complement face-to-face classes.

Does this Sound like Fraud to You?

Dean Duffy decided that his strategic plan this year would include a professional certification program of four web-based courses. Each of these four courses appearing on the face-to-face course schedule would be taught by four different senior professors. Instead of asking those faculty members to transition their courses to online formats, he elected to offer that task of designing all four courses to a junior professor and an adjunct instructor. Each claimed to know how to produce quality online courses. Although new to online learning, the dean anticipated a large market for this new online certification program state-wide.

Scott and Bob teamed up to compile courses that in some instances covered material out of their collective areas of expertise. In fact, they farmed out some of the work to newly minted graduates from the institution's doctoral program. In a short time, Scott and Bob showed the four completed courses to the dean for his approval. Ecstatic and proud, Dean Duffy announced to his faculty at the general fall meeting that the courses now appeared online.

Adjuncts including Paul facilitated one of these courses. About eight weeks into the semester, however, Paul resigned from the institution prompting Duffy to ask the senior faculty member who taught that course face-to-face if she would facilitate the online course, too. Despite a busy schedule, Debbie agreed when Duffy assured her that the adjunct had monitored all work thus far and mid-semester grades were up to date.

Once in the course shell, Debbie discovered that Paul had done nothing. His visibility could not be found in any of the discussion boards. She found no grades in the online grade book. Livid, Debbie marched into Duffy's office for an explanation. Reluctantly, Duffy told Debbie that Paul was collecting disability and the watchdogs discovered that he was teaching this course. Debbie shot back with the fact that, indeed, Paul was not doing anything in this course. Duffy agreed to compensate her for her trouble and begged her to facilitate the course for the remainder of the semester. With apprehension, Debbie agreed.

As if the adjunct situation wasn't enough to trouble her, Debbie began to sink her teeth into the course only to discover that the content and quality of the course her colleagues, Scott and Bob, assembled proved woefully lacking. Debbie concerned herself with the fact that the poor quality of this online course may place students in jeopardy of passing the certification exam. Debbie began to wonder if the other three courses under the guidance of Scott and Bob also tended to be of poor quality.

Once again she marched into Duffy's office with her concerns. Duffy back-pedaled and tap-danced around the issues and assured her the other courses were fine. A glance at the enrollment for them indicated that regardless of quality, each course proved to be a consistent money maker.

Online courses possess the potential to eclipse face-to-face courses when they are done correctly, maintain rigor and high quality, and engage students in the material using the best features of the technology available. When faculty or administration view online delivery as a means to increase revenue, an occasion to hire more adjuncts, and an opportunity to capture a market niche, then online delivery can compromise learning.

Neither of the characters in this vignette knew anything about online delivery despite their entry into it. For the dean to initiate an online program without knowledge of it appears short-sighted. He needed to know what he was getting into, what support he needed to ensure a quality program, who best to task with the development and delivery of the program, and where his market could be found, among other things. Opportunists Scott and Bob took advantage of the situation and the dean's lack of knowledge of online delivery to carve their own professional niche. They convinced him erroneously that they possessed the necessary skill and technical savvy to get the job done.

Hiring Paul without a background check indicated that Scott or Bob or the dean recommended him and none realized his situation or knew about his disability status. They may have assumed that no one would find out about that status. Learning was compromised until Debbie performed her own quality control. Had she not, students completing the four-course sequence may have experienced difficulty passing their licensure exam, which could have created more problems for the dean. But Debbie also knew nothing about online delivery. Fortunately, however, she did know about integrity and quality and what should be taught in the courses, especially hers. As this house of cards fell due to poor leadership and administration, Debbie demonstrated her dedication to her program and role as faculty.

Sadly the driving force in the development of the courses and the program seemed to be financial in nature. The dean measured success by the bottom line;

Scott and Bob measured success by how quickly and cheaply they assembled and staffed the courses; and Debbie measured success by quality courses that led to student learning and the successful completion of the exam. If the dean saw web-based instruction as a potential strategic move for his school to deliver a certificate/license, he was obliged to pursue that with integrity. Offering professional development and hands-on training to the four senior professors to design the courses seems like a more logical way to approach the task. Eventually, that scenario played out but it likely cost the program more in time and financial resources to fix the problems Scott and Bob caused than to do it right in the first place. Duffy must also recognize that what is being delivered in the content of those courses constitutes quality instruction and his lack of knowledge precluded him from assessing the whole situation. Teams of faculty, instructional technology, and instructional design personnel can ensure the quality control needed to produce solid web-based courses.

DEBRIEFING TEACHING ONLINE

Historian Arthur Schlesinger (n.d.) wrote, "Science and technology revolutionize our lives, but memory, tradition, and myth frame our response." The teaching to learning paradigm predicted nearly 20 years ago by Barr and Tagg (1995) came to fruition with online delivery. In 2010, student enrollment in online courses topped 6.1 million students. Web-based course growth rates now far exceed on-campus enrollment growth (Allen & Seaman, 2011). Online delivery arrived, however, with frustration, apprehension, and some entrepreneurial opportunism. Because of technology, instructional delivery has changed. However, adapting to initial advances and new learning technologies, although utterly fascinating as a result of its adaptive nature, still creates consternation among faculty and administrators (Schneckenberg, 2009). Wickersham and McElhany (2010) learned that faculty contemplating teaching online seemingly became more concerned with how teaching online would affect them *personally* rather than affect the program or the students *academically*.

Christensen and Eyring (2011) refer to online learning as a disruptive innovation. Web-based learning became the purview of the for-profit institutions that attempted to improve upon the traditional delivery of post-secondary education. Unfortunately for the not-for-profit counterparts, the competition to improve upon their first several hundred years of traditional instruction did not always result in drastic improvements. Higher education evolves naturally and becomes responsive to changes tried at the most prestigious institutions like Harvard, for instance. Typically, what works well at some types of institutions fails miserably when copied and implemented at others.

According to Weick (1976), universities are loosely coupled systems to which administrations can discontinue or add new functions, thus making online delivery fairly easy to implement. However, movement into web-based education necessitates a structural as well as cultural change. Surface changes affecting the administrative structure combine with shifts in perceiving curriculum and delivering course content in the academic culture. Adding the administration is one issue; tinkering with centuries of traditional philosophical and pedagogical course delivery is quite another (Mitchell, 2009). Therefore, administrators often become the scapegoat when they make decisions regarding online learning that are devoid of dialog, discussion, or debate with their faculty. These instances force galvanization of issues, ideologies, and people siding with one platform or the other due to pedagogical stance, political allegiance, and even fear (Harris & Hartley, 2011). In institutions that reward research over teaching, pushing for online course options often marginalizes this initiative. Deciding to move courses to online formats includes managing new e-learning strategies and technologies and understanding their instructive potential as well as providing the financing and training for web-based instruction (Schneckenberg, 2009).

The push to capture online niches and market shares or to offer convenience to learners often propels administrators to jump on the bandwagon, albeit ill-equipped and lacking in knowledge about the medium (Rice & Miller, 2001). Strategies for synchronous and asynchronous delivery can be adapted to target underserved student populations in remote geographic locations as well as to transmit conventional subjects in unconventional ways, which are positive things. In these vignettes faculty seems willing to embrace web-based instruction but the situations highlight the fact that administrations often offer online courses before their programs and faculty are ready. In the absence of laying the necessary groundwork or offering continued support, administrators encountered difficulty in several areas despite the fact that Dean Duffy's program made money.

Online education needs planned change and lead time to implement it properly. Online policies devised by faculty in conjunction with administration and staff tend to work better. Administrative change encompasses more procedural matters when transitioning to online but it may mean imposing something foreign onto existing, deeply engrained or archaic administrative mindsets. These administrative concerns include admissions, registration, tuition differentials, targeted marketing strategies, faculty course loads, intellectual property rights, and compensation expectations. As a result, administrators should actually take (and teach) an online course to understand the process and the changes that faculty will undergo to make that transition (Ferdig & Dawson, 2006; Mitchell, 2009; Orr, Williams, & Pennington, 2009).

Romeu (2002/2003) encouraged administrators to raise faculty morale rather than ignore it by providing additional options to those who choose to teach online. He suggested that colleges provide ongoing faculty development, more opportunities for faculty to teach other faculty about online delivery, and occasional course releases to give faculty time to prepare courses, and that they extend graduate student assistance, and encourage peer reviewing of existing courses to further best practices. In addition, Cook, Ley, Crawford, and Warner (2009) added that external motivation to sustain their efforts in the form of technical support, tangible monetary rewards, and better training would also be welcome. Faculty training exists at more than 90 percent of the online course providers; most offer mentoring and in-house training (Allen & Seaman, 2011; Mitchell, 2009).

Rice and Miller (2001) cautioned that "the failure to develop a framework for planning for the use and integration of technology has the potential to prove costly in both competition and financial terms" (p. 329). These researchers also realized that as faculty become savvy working collaboratively with instructional technicians and designers, they will need to have a voice in administrative matters such as in what course management system to invest.

THE REST OF THE STORY

Diane, her colleagues, and her savvy chair unraveled the issues that appeared to be thwarting their efforts to promote a doctoral program. Armed with documentation and information from other doctoral programs at the institution, they learned their program was taking a lethal blow. Their collective efforts caused the admissions person to be replaced, the provost to be forced to resign, and the IT department to create best practice models and assist faculty on a continual basis. A year following Sherri's comments to her colleagues about the need for full-time instructional design support to assist faculty creating and teaching online courses, the college hired professional staff to assist professors at University B. Sherri seeks out their assistance quite often. But she has no idea if other faculty utilize this new staff or if the presence of the staff encourages other faculty members to teach online or incorporate online components into their classes. Debbie learned from a colleague in another part of the state that Scott and Bob marketed their skills to other institutions as part of a consulting business they initiated. They sought to develop similar courses like the four they developed originally. Subsequently, Debbie revamped another of the courses in the sequence. Eventually, the dean hired a faculty member highly skilled in online course development and delivery to assist faculty who teach online.

BEST PRACTICES

- Online course development and delivery is complicated. Faculty need to know they have IT staff in place to assist them before they transition their courses. Using a knowledgeable, trained faculty person to oversee colleague involvement in this process is strongly recommended. Faculty will listen to and appreciate faculty peers rather than interact only with IT professionals as they transition to online delivery.

- Faculty should incorporate online delivery into programs and courses because the use of the medium enhances learning. This philosophy engenders the correct approach to course development. To push online delivery to increase market share, target new markets, or offer convenience of learning rarely entices faculty to join the movement. These may only increase angst among faculty, and devalue programs if they lack rigor and quality.

- Faculty should formulate explicit policies and procedures for online instruction in accordance with accreditation guidelines and legal constraints in order to achieve quality outcomes (Wickersham & McElhany, 2010).

- Faculty must know their options and existing resources before making the final decision to teach online. Faculty need ongoing professional development in this area, a supportive IT team, and fellow colleagues engaging in the same practices with whom they can interact. Without these, faculty will struggle.

RESOURCES

- For faculty new to online, how-to books abound on designing online courses, maximizing hybrid courses that combine classroom with online options, teaching options in synchronous or asynchronous formats, engaging students in online discussion formats, and utilizing the medium to bring out the best in a course. Academic book publishers often provide a series of such texts that should be made available to faculty by the dean. *Best Practices for Teaching with Emerging Technologies* by Michelle Pacansky-Brock (2012) summarizes what faculty need to know.

- Campus IT departments possess the information and resources faculty need to begin as well as stay current in online delivery. Having IT people on staff to work with faculty in their courses gives faculty comfort and ensures that they are doing their best to affect learning. York and Vance (2009) suggested that online support teams include a librarian to connect course goals to vital online library resources. Like instructional technology staff, librarians may enroll in the class in order to better serve the student and instructor as well as supply immediate troubleshooting capabilities or information on copyright issues.

- Information from Educause may be helpful, as they are a non-profit organization that advances higher learning through information technology. They offer a variety of services, publish an online journal, hold conferences, and support blogs and wikis to assist faculty teaching online and can be located at www.educause.edu/ero/article/myth-about-online-course-development.

Chapter 5
Departmental Culture
Expect the Unexpected

INTRODUCTION

Each faculty department on every campus possesses its own exceptional character. No two departmental cultures resemble each other. They tend to be unique creations molded and shaped by their distinctive faculty. Disciplines and professional fields attract specific types of men and women who become further socialized into those departments (Weidman et al., 2001). As a result departments exhibit quirks, habits, idiosyncrasies, standards, and modes of behavior exclusive to them. While one colleague may describe her department as a community another may regard it as family. A community of practice implies that all members reside on equal footing and contribute to the whole, while the family analogy implies a one-way descending hierarchy and power structure. Functional departments tend to follow the community of practice model while the dysfunctional department claims the same approach but more than likely follows the patriarchal family model in practice.

  Departments must be efficient in order to function properly. In order to determine departmental efficiency, "quantities of outputs produced and inputs used in the academic process must be collected and compared with ideals or benchmark performance criteria" (Tauer, Fried, & Fry, 2007, p. 473). In this way, inefficient departments can determine new strategic direction and formulate policy to facilitate better, more efficient outcomes. Inputs consist of budgeted funds and the allocation of faculty time distributed across prescribed percentages of teaching, research, and service. These differ by institution, department, and faculty within them. Outputs include credit-hour generation, number and amount of contracts and grants, and faculty publication productivity.

  Managing scarce resources requires greater efficiency. Maintaining departmental efficiency and viability in the face of declining resources poses challenges to chairs, deans, and faculty. Minimizing dysfunction of any kind aids in greater efficiency and also contributes to departmental effectiveness (Tauer et al., 2007).

Effective departments employ faculty who work together or function collegially to carry out the mission, goals, purpose, and vision for the department. More often than not, however, factors like power misalignment, politics, personality and ideological conflicts create dysfunction within a department.

Faculty in departments may be unaware of the dysfunction that occurs over an extended period of time. They may facilitate it or become a part of it rather than be resistant to established practice. New faculty members to a department may view this established practice as odd or quirky or even dysfunctional (Hall, 2002). However, it becomes difficult for novices to penetrate an existing culture and power structure without assuming risk as a result of their precarious, untenured position (Jawitz, 2007).

Trying to construct a professional identity and career to seamlessly weave oneself into the department fabric takes time, effort, and good perception. New faculty may easily spot dysfunction when they enter a department (Hall, 2002) and not know what to do about it. Perceptions obtained by new academics, that is, ways they construct their reality of the department, can run contrary to how the department functions in reality. An array of conflicting messages given off by senior faculty and administration can further confound a faculty member new to the department (Jawitz, 2007).

Faculty can escape or ignore the dysfunction by isolating themselves physically and emotionally and concentrating on their research and teaching expectations. However, monthly faculty meetings tend to bring out the best and worst in faculty as they gather with the department chair/head to discuss faculty business. While attendance is expected, participation may not be, especially from the untenured faculty. Some faculty may take the time seriously; others grade papers during the meeting. Some meetings are occasions for seeing colleagues and catching up; other meetings can be filled with politics, posturing, and contention depending upon the agenda. Department business and faculty meetings in the following vignettes cover various topics and show multiple faculty demeanors but one common character threads through all the vignettes. The presence of one unsavory personality can negatively affect functionality but the faculty that continues to ignore the behavior engrains a dysfunctional culture unresponsive to change.

Vulgarity and Insensitivity

One would presume that this Friday faculty meeting would not be different from the others but oddly it proved to be. Debate heated the room over the dean's proposal to fold six existing departments in the college into four. Each department had to make a case for their survival. The discussion then focused on what this particular department would say to convince the dean they should be one of the four left standing. During the discussion, a senior professor responded to a comment made by a new faculty member

DEPARTMENTAL CULTURE

with a vulgar retort. Hal's reply: "If we do not make our case using my approach, we will end up sucking hind tit." Faculty members present in the meeting were noticeably aghast at the comment. No one said anything at the time.

As the meeting drew to a close, Hal presented a small wrapped package to a colleague in the meeting who was having his 65th birthday that day. An avid golfer, Glenn realized that the package contained golf balls and tees and he appeared very appreciative. With closer examination, faculty around him realized that the golf balls had vulgar comments on them. In front of his colleagues, Glenn threw the package in the trash but only after Hal had already exited the meeting. Nothing more was said.

Hal saw this meeting as an opportunity to embarrass his colleague under the disguise of birthday humor. But first, he expressed himself in a vulgar and inappropriate manner to everyone. Both of these behaviors are unacceptable on several levels, including violating propriety, insulting the women (and men) in the group, and taking inappropriate personal liberties in a professional setting. However, the worst offense committed that day is that *no one* spoke up in the meeting to castigate Hal for either of his actions when they happened. Neither the chair nor faculty colleagues said a word of admonishment to Hal. Even Glenn, who had been insulted the most, never rebuked Hal for his childish prank. Furthermore, no one required Hal to apologize; no one held him accountable. By keeping silent, Hal's behavior continued.

Because of the power Hal held within the department given his tenure and time in rank as a full professor, he used it unabashedly to say and do whatever he wanted. He knew no one *would* say anything. They never had before. Then again, he believed that he was well within his rights given his rank and status to say anything. Unless someone takes Hal to task, and immediacy is important here, he will live to strike another day.

Hazing of New Faculty Members

As is typical of new faculty until they achieve tenure, some remain silent in meetings especially during controversial discussions. Unfortunately, one new member, Dale, never received that memo and challenged the senior patriarch of the department, Hal. After Hal offered his point of view on the matter, Hal added that his suggestion for dealing with the issue at hand appeared consistent with the way things were always done in the department. Dale asked politely, "Why is that, Hal? Why do we have to do things a certain way all the time? Why can't we try different ways?" Hal flashed a curious, icy stare at Dale.

When the meeting adjourned, faculty members headed to their respective offices. Dale sauntered to the departmental mail room to check his box. Hal followed Dale into the mail room and pinned him to the wall. In no uncertain terms, Hal told Dale, "Never challenge me or embarrass me in a faculty meeting ever again."

Dale had every right to question Hal about *his* plan for the department. Acting collegially, Dale posed the question as a newcomer who simply did not understand why the department had to do things one way only. Dale's tenure in the department did not yet afford him insight into the prevailing culture. Other options, Dale reasoned, had to exist and the faculty needed to explore them. Dale attempted to make sense of the department reality that appeared quite unusual to him as a newcomer to the department.

For Hal to act the way he did toward Dale shows his behavior to be far from collegial. In fact, Hal again allowed the bully in him to emerge at Dale's expense, shock, and surprise. After all, Dale's first faculty meeting should be a welcoming experience not a battleground for the new versus old guard.

What transpired in the faculty meeting following Dale's comment shocked the faculty who never challenged Hal either. To have a new faculty member stand up to Hal was unfortunate given that tenured faculty avoided him. It was too soon for Dale to get a grip on the department political playground and power differential. Dale had no idea what he had done. Hal should have been more forgiving of the newcomer. What is unconscionable, however, is the fact that no faculty came to Dale's rescue during this meeting. They sat in silence allowing Dale to take the brunt of Hal's anger. Surely the faculty in residence knew that Hal would not let Dale's comment go unpunished. Even the chair of the department had to know that Hal would not let Dale's probe slip by unnoticed. Yet no one came to Dale's rescue to support his query during the meeting or immediately after it. Hal chose a public place to confront Dale but no one ventured into the mail room until after the physical confrontation.

Welcome to the Department

As a new assistant professor straight out of her PhD program, Toni settled into her office comfortably. The senior professor in the next office, Cindy, commented on how quickly she had moved in and unpacked. Toni informed Cindy that the married couple in the department, Hal and Jane, helped her not only move into her office but into her apartment as well. They supplied her with several home-cooked meals to show her their hospitality. This confirmed to Toni that she made the correct decision to begin her professional career here. Cindy cautioned Toni that while these things appeared to be wonderful gestures, she knew the couple well enough to know that at some point they would be back to collect. Toni dismissed Cindy's prediction.

Months passed before Toni knocked on Cindy's door. Toni seemed upset, so Cindy dropped what she was doing. Toni said she had just returned from a conference where she, Hal, and Jane had presented a co-authored paper. Toni did all of the research and writing, but they told Toni that because they mentored her and helped her network within this professional organization, their names needed to be on the paper presentation first. During the conference session, the couple presented the paper as if it was theirs while Toni sat silent. Toni told Cindy that she wished she had listened to her earlier.

Cindy comforted Toni by telling her that she was not the first to fall victim to the couple. Years before, they did the same thing to the new department chair. He sang their praises to Cindy one day and Cindy gave him the same warning she offered Toni. He did not believe Cindy either. Months later, the chair called Cindy into his office to offer her an apology. While they did not steal his work, they sold him out when he did not give them something for which they had asked. Toni asked Cindy if other faculty in the department knew about Hal's and Jane's behavior pattern with new faculty and administration. Cindy acknowledged that they undoubtedly did.

Let's give Cindy credit for some helpful informal mentoring regardless of the fact that neither Toni, nor the department chair, heeded her advice. Other people in the department knew of the married couple's behavior pattern and although Cindy may not have been the only person warning the chair, she *was* the only person to tell Toni of the consequences arising from the couple's actions. To take advantage of new faculty and administrators in order to benefit personally or professionally seems unconscionable but few members of the department addressed the issue or succeeded in stopping their behavior.

Hal and Jane maintained self-proclaimed power in the department. They had no authority but they wielded power as a result of their tenured rank and full status. As a coalition, they used that power to sway others. Faculty decided perhaps to overlook their manipulations until they reached full tenured professor status themselves. Given the depth and breadth of their power, they gravitated to new colleagues like the department chair and Toni because they satisfied a need or supplied a benefit to the couple and these folks would be naïve enough to take the bait.

DEBRIEFING THE DEPARTMENTAL CULTURE

New faculty enter a new culture into which they must become acculturated and acclimated. Seasoned faculty seems obliged to mentor new faculty and assist them with this process (Davis, 2001; Heggins, 2004; Tillman, 2011). Literature on mentoring indicates its positive effects on junior faculty (Zellers, Howard, & Barcic, 2008). But, many senior faculty have little or no time to devote to junior faculty mentoring, may possess little skill or ability with regard to mentoring, or offer unstructured opportunities for junior faculty that seem more hit and miss than effective opportunities to ease new faculty into the department (Borders et al., 2011; Eddy & Gaston-Gayles, 2008;Thomas & Gillespie, 2008). Some chairs have been known to assign senior faculty to junior faculty and encourage them to be mentors. These assignments must be revisited periodically to assess progress and/or contemplate reassignment (Foote, 2009; Pololi, 2005).

Often junior faculty seek out mentors but without knowing the departmental landscape, and thus have to leave it to chance of whether they find the best possible person for the task. In the Jawitz (2007) study junior faculty felt that they received little support from senior faculty. This forced them to find a formal or informal mentor or confidant to ease their entry. Still other faculty learned where the landmines were buried by observing colleagues and, then, treading lightly. For instance, Jawitz found that old guard faculty practices and expectations for teaching and research must be communicated to new faculty. However, what the old guard expects is not always what they currently practice. This sends conflicting messages to junior faculty trying to acclimate.

By all indications, Dale had no mentor to explain the culture to him. He jeopardized his position in the department when he questioned those in power and intimated that there must be a better way (Bedeian, 2002). When the chair realized that Dale made a major faux pas during the meeting, he should have talked to Dale personally. The chair knew Hal well enough to know Dale may have placed himself in professional jeopardy. If the chair could not find a willing mentor for Dale, the chair needed to assume that role himself. Cindy served as an informal mentor to Toni supplying her with valuable information. However, Toni was convinced that the married couple, Hal and Jane, had proven to be the best mentors she could have found. In fact, *they* found her. If Toni had little idea what the expectations were from a mentor, she would be easily fooled by Hal and Jane. Their actions focused on Toni's personal comforts rather than her professional development. It took a semester before she realized that they had their own best interests at heart, not hers. Hal and Jane took a cherished bond of mentor/mentee and used it to deceive Toni and feather their bed. Now what recourse does Toni as an untenured professor have against the most powerful collective force in the department?

Toni and Dale know first-hand that they may be powerless against these departmental forces. Glenn had full tenure status but he chose to ignore Hal's behavior as did other tenured faculty in the department. Because the chair of this department had authority to override some of this power, he needed to exercise it on behalf of these junior and senior colleagues but no evidence exists to show that. In fact, he too fell victim to their shenanigans. Toni talked to Cindy but we have no indication that Toni or Dale or Glenn sought assistance from their department chair or another faculty member. No other faculty member came to their aid publically. The imbalance of power wielded by Hal indicates that it had reached a level that strikes fear in most everyone attached to the situation such that no one acts but simply looks the other way. Clearly, Hal exhibits bullying behavior and along with his spouse created a bully culture within the department (Namie & Namie, 2000; Twale & De Luca, 2008). Even though Cindy aired her comments to Toni and the department chair, the chair did not go so far as to address the problem even after he became aware of his own victimization. The chair and the faculty by their complacence allowed a bully culture to flourish and the resulting dysfunction affected other members of the department.

New faculty, with or without the help of a mentor/confidant, must assess the power structure and differential within the department. Like an anthropologist studying a foreign culture, new faculty must do the same (Nathan, 2005; Twale & De Luca, 2008) in order to ensure their own individual success. Not every department embodies the engrained dysfunction this one does, but Toni and Dale had no idea a bully culture prevailed until after they took the position.

New faculty must establish a professional identity through their socialization process. That identity harbors components of teaching, research, and service. If the academic culture indicates that research eclipses teaching, new faculty would be wise to develop their professional persona around honed research, presentation, and publication and find a mentor to assist them or ask their chair to help them find one. To focus on teaching and service would create an identity contrary to the established research norm and the short (merit pay) and long (tenure and promotion) results would be counterproductive (Jawitz, 2007). Neither Dale nor Toni had been members of the department long enough to begin this quest, a quest that requires time, patience, observation, and interview.

Inquiring civilly and discretely about the 'elephant in the room' and understanding its presence could go a long way to reducing its size and impact. To confront the elephant suddenly and head on will only anger the beast and its keepers (Hall, 2002). With such precarious beginnings in the department, there is little to no reason for Dale or Toni to want to do that. Hal and Jane supplied a smoke-and-mirrors approach to mentoring Toni. Hal baptized Dale with fire not water. As the most vulnerable citizens of the department, Dale and Toni needed protection from the beginning and not much was forthcoming despite the knowledge the department faculty and chair had regarding Hal and Jane. In Glenn's case, faculty expected him to take care of himself as he had as much clout as Hal.

THE REST OF THE STORY

A few years after the birthday gift incident, Glenn retired. Hal stayed on and continued to say and do what he wanted. Dale spent his second semester on the faculty searching for and finding another faculty position. He never spoke up in another meeting or tarried long in the mail room. Toni spent her third year on campus searching for and finding another faculty position. During that time she avoided Hal and Jane. This couple spent another 15 years on the faculty before retiring. Cindy informed another faculty member about Hal and Jane, and she, too, failed to heed the warning. However, she acknowledged to Cindy years later that she wished she had.

BEST PRACTICES

- As a new faculty member, tenured or untenured, socialization into the department is essential. To accomplish that, faculty must study the departmental climate, observe faculty behavior and relationships, interview colleagues as a way to understand the environment, and make sense of it to successfully maneuver through the culture.

- Faculty preparing graduate students for academe would be wise to include socialization, acclimation, and enculturation as part of their formal and informal curricula. Practicing collegiality in graduate school may go a long way to successful socialization as new faculty. Reflection rather than critique is one way to evaluate others' work more civilly (Hall, 2002).

- New faculty often expose their vulnerability inadvertently to predators. Cohorts of entering junior faculty should be formed to bridge their isolation and assist with their socialization. Junior faculty need to interact with peers as well as locate a mentor or mentors with whom they feel comfortable. Untenured faculty need to ask around before assuming that the first colleague on the doorstep possesses genuine interest in their professional development.

- As tenured faculty members, challenge injustices perpetrated by caustic colleagues as a means to identify and reverse dysfunction. Faculty should bring their concerns before chairs/heads and deans who also need to deal with dysfunction rather than ignore it. Faculty must be encouraged to speak up or speak out and not ignore the elephant in the room. Also recommended is not having married couples in the same department if it can be avoided.

- Colleges and universities should appoint an ombudsperson who focuses on faculty issues. Faculty positioned at all ranks should be familiar with the ombudsperson, the duties and parameters of the role, and seek assistance from this office when they need it.

RESOURCES

- Twale and De Luca (2008) in *Faculty Incivility* offered suggestions for dealing with incivility in academe. Donald Hall (2002) posited additional counsel for new faculty in his *The Academic Self: An Owner's Manual. Professors Behaving Badly* by John Braxton (2011) should offer the reader further assistance. Should faculty and administrators need clearly stated guidelines to help them deal with less than collegial faculty, the AAUP's website contains valuable information (www.aaup.org/issues-higher-education).

- Various generic book titles exist on how to manage regular people, difficult people, technical people, and negative people as well as how to manage stress and conflict in the workplace. Familiar authors who discuss leadership and management include Kenneth Blanchard, Peter Drucker, John Bennett, Lee Bolman, and Deryl Leaming. Recent titles related to managing faculty, specifically, include *Working with Problem Faculty* (2012), *Reframing Academic Leadership* (2011), *The Department Chair Primer* (2006), and *Faculty Stress* (2009).

- Several large campuses employ faculty ombudspersons to assist faculty. Several websites examples listed below should provide enough information to encourage faculty to value this campus resource as well as provide academic administrators with suggestions on how to appoint an officer to set up a department for their campus faculty: the University of South Carolina at www.sc.edu/ombuds/; the Ohio State University at http://ombudsman.osu.edu/; and Trinity College at www.trincoll.edu/prog/facman/doc0006.html.

Chapter 6
On the Tenure Track

INTRODUCTION

Undoubtedly, the greatest concern for new faculty is not class size, distance between office door and parking space, or research agenda, but rather promotion and tenure (P&T). Achieving promotion and tenure consumes junior faculty energy for the first five, six, or seven years of their professional career. It may be easier on junior faculty if the document describing P&T procedures and the faculty presiding over the P&T committee interpreted the document identically and consistently. It may be helpful if the senior faculty discussed it with new faculty . . . *period*. Often untenured faculty shy from asking their tenured colleagues for this much needed assistance. Of the junior faculty who do ask for help, they find that different senior faculty colleagues offer different subjective judgments of what it takes to secure tenure and that may differ from advice given by the department chair or advice shared with other junior colleagues in the same or neighboring departments.

Tenure promises the university a stable faculty upon which it can depend from semester to semester. That implies that tenure may have stronger economic than intellectual implications (Burgan, 2003). However, faculty formulate the documents with intellectual quality standards in mind more than with a desire to meet administrative economic needs (Plater, 1998). Unfortunately, most P&T documents are written vaguely and, thus, remain open to interpretation and legal challenge by faculty, departments, and institutions. Asking several colleagues may yield several responses that can range from accurate to misleading to confusing.

Faculty candidates must demonstrate their citizenship in the department, college, and university when the university awards or extends tenure to them (Plater, 1998). A professor's ability to be collegial may or may not be part of the tenure process, however. Some colleges completely ignore collegiality while others use it in ways that make it difficult to arrive at a definitive faculty vote. In other words, some faculty members compile prolific records of teaching and especially research and publication but are not particularly well suited to collaborative work. Other faculty work well on committees but often experience difficulties homing in on a research agenda, conducting research, presenting at conferences, or subsequently being successful at finding homes for their scholarship in acceptable peer-reviewed journals.

Sorting through the academic materials objectively and assessing the more subjectively based category of collegiality creates a conundrum for many P&T committee members. Silverman (2004) quipped, "Departments 'get even' with faculty who are considered to be severely lacking in collegiality by not supporting them strongly when they are considered for promotion . . . [and] a lack of support sometimes is intended to send a strong message that the person should change or leave" (p. 9). By the same token one may also extrapolate that non-collegial voters may be put off by a collegial colleague. Collegiality prospers when faculty practice collaboration through mentoring, scholarly research and writing, team teaching, and committee work (Lenze, 1999).

Academic freedom and tenure allow faculty to pursue their intellectual interests and research agenda as well as teach the 'truth' specified by their particular field or discipline (Austin & Rice, 1998; Plater, 1998). New faculty are often cautioned to walk on eggshells until they can discern if their agendas will be acceptable to their colleagues. The Theda Skocpol case of the 1980s lent credibility to the notion that if colleagues assessing your tenure do not like your line of inquiry, or your gender for that matter, it could surely jeopardize your chances of securing their support (Jacobs, 2006).

Tenure also offers faculty members the academic freedom to criticize or be critical of administrative policy, direction, and governance. Academic freedom can also be characterized as encouraging dissent, be it among faculty peers or with administration. In any case, it should occur without penalty to the challenger (Slevin, 2000). These privileges should not give license to junior faculty to be disrespectful, unethical, or uncivil to peers and administrators, however (Stimpson, 2000), as there is a distinct difference (Twale & De Luca, 2008).

The tenure and promotion process typically begins with a pre-tenure review usually in the junior faculty member's third year on the faculty. Credentials may be reviewed separately in research institutions for junior faculty seeking graduate faculty status. Tenure review varies by university from only one opportunity to two opportunities and candidates may be eligible as early as their fourth year and as late as their seventh year (Austin & Rice, 1998). New hires with five, six, or more years of previous experience may receive a two-year 'up or out' contract and, therefore, must achieve tenure rather quickly.

For many faculty members the road to tenure is smooth and uneventful but, for others, it is bumpy and laden with unanticipated obstacles, orange barrels, and potholes (Lang, 2005; Sorcinelli, 2002). Those obstacles can be inherent in the junior faculty member who fails to acclimate well to academe or fails to become acculturated. Roadblocks may also be the result of faculty and administration who fail to socialize new candidates, mentor them, and do what is necessary to ensure their success. Miller, Brueggeman, Blue, and Shephard (1997) examined graduate students regarding these students' perceptions of their preparation for the faculty role of assistant professor. While students felt comfortable in their ability to teach and perhaps conduct research, they knew little to nothing about campus organization, policies, or the faculty–administrative relationship. If new junior faculty hires expect to receive clarification or hand-holding once they move into an office and begin teaching, they may be surprised to learn that acclimating new faculty to university life is not, unfortunately, a top priority of their senior colleagues. Lip service may be paid but mentoring could be sporadic, haphazard, and ineffective, to the detriment of junior colleagues. The following case vignettes offer insight into the path to tenure beginning with the pre-tenure process.

Dana's Pre-tenure Review

It was time for Dana's third year pre-tenure review. Not to worry, she had published a few articles and demonstrated that she would continue to do so. Her teaching evaluations ranked above many seasoned professors in her department and program. She performed enough service functions in her department and in the college to suffice. The university also considered collegiality part of the tenure equation. Unfortunately, the tenure document presented a vague definition for collegiality. Dana's department seemed to value congeniality but often confused it with the real definition of collegiality.

When the department head's letter chronicling the meeting on Dana's pre-tenure review arrived in her mailbox, Dana read it with curiosity. The department faculty lauded her efforts in teaching, research, and service as she had expected. However, the final paragraph on collegiality sat in her stomach like a stack of buckwheat pancakes, especially the summary sentence, which read, "We feel we don't know you." To be sure of the implications of this information, Dana shared her letter with her graduate assistant, who was a former lawyer. He indicated the faculty clearly confused congeniality with collegiality. He suggested that she write a letter to the department chair asking for ways that 'knowing me' could be facilitated among the department faculty. Dana waited for a verbal or written response. One never came.

Designed to be a formative evaluation, pre-tenure review helps the candidate of three years determine if he or she is on track, slightly off track, or way off track. It allows enough time for candidates to find their bearings and reassess their plan for tenure, keep going with full speed, or reevaluate their career choice or institutional selection and/or search for another job. Dana's letter included information on her teaching, research, and service. From that she determined she was on track and poised to move in the direction she had been going. Her colleagues affirmed her strong candidacy for tenure. Dana demonstrated that her work aligned well with the standards posted in the university tenure and promotion document.

Because collegiality is not always considered important by some university faculties but regarded as highly important to others, a vague definition further confounds the candidate. Just because a definition is contained in the P&T document does not mean that the interpretation, spirit, or operationalization of that definition spans all institutions, departments, or faculty members over time or discipline. The definition or spirit of collegiality can be manipulated in such a way as to tenure someone who demonstrates poor performance in teaching and research but is a colleague whom everyone 'likes.' By the same token, collegiality can serve to oust someone whose abrasive personality or research interest does not fit well with colleagues but whose tenure dossier appears impressive.

In Dana's case she may have spent too much time doing the work she was expected to do. Perhaps she failed to mingle at the water cooler or arrive early to spend an hour each morning sitting in the faculty room smoking, chatting, and drinking her morning coffee with her colleagues. The faculty may have had good intentions to weave Dana into the culture of the department but did not realize she committed herself to her work rather than what she considered idle socializing. Perhaps neither Dana nor the faculty had a clear interpretation of what was expected 'collegially' of them or her. *Had* Dana explored the definition of collegiality and operationalized it, there would be no guarantee that her colleagues would have recognized it similarly. Their definition or the spirit in which they couched collegiality in *their* 'departmental culture' proved to be different.

Dana's goals differed perhaps from her colleagues who were already tenured and also of those nearing retirement. They may have been coasting along and she 'hit the ground running' and operated in overdrive. Her plan would be to stay that way given the positive assessment of her teaching, research, and service. Coasting was not an option.

The original letter from the department head should have included more information on collegiality, including the P&T definition, how important it was to securing tenure, and how the department culture interpreted it. The essence of the faculty assessment and discussion on collegiality should have been captured in the chair's letter in order to give Dana clear guidelines for addressing her colleagues' concerns. That she sought counsel from her lawyer graduate assistant proved a wise move. That she followed his advice and asked for clarification on the matter was an even wiser move. However, the failure of the department chair to respond in writing to her request indicated poor administrative procedure and judgment on his part. According to Dana's graduate assistant, the chair's failure to respond would have been an issue should she not receive tenure in a few years. He indicated that, as a result of this oversight, she had grounds to appeal a future negative tenure decision.

Doral's Graduate Faculty Status

In order to chair dissertations, Doral had to make Level 2 graduate faculty status by the end of his fourth year. This achievement was exacting in that he had to have four scholarly, research-based, refereed publications (quantitative or qualitative) in first, second, or third tier refereed journals. Journal publication acceptance rates in those journals needed to be less than 50 percent, however, while 33 percent or less would be better (see Cabell's Directories in your library reference section or online). Most of the articles needed to have the candidate as the first or only author. Doral had the four peer-reviewed articles that he needed but they did not necessarily meet the latter expectations. In fact three of the four articles he wrote appeared in journals that ranked above the 50 percent acceptance mark, closer to 75 percent acceptance rate. He was the first author on one and the second and third author on the others.

During the meeting it became clear that a few senior colleagues supported Doral and a few did not. The remainder of the faculty silently waited to render their vote in a paper ballot. While one colleague indicated that the quality of Doral's work needed to be better, the senior colleague opposition said that Doral had a wife and child to support and had recently bought a house in town. University policy stated that a 'no' vote would mean an automatic dismissal from the university at the close of the semester as Level 2 status was necessary for tenure. A candidate had only one attempt to achieve Level 2 status. These senior faculty members pleaded that a 'no' vote would place him and his family in dire financial circumstances. One female colleague stated that Doral, unfortunately and clearly, did not meet quality standards, set forth by the university, for graduate faculty status. The senior faculty members argued with the female colleague who pushed for quality. They indicated that she clearly had a vendetta against Doral and wanted him out. This was her chance. The final vote favored Doral by a 12 to 2 margin.

While we can feel sympathy for Doral's plight, the decision to award or deny status rested on the specified guidelines and how closely his work measured against those written standards of quality. In this case, his work did not meet those standards on multiple counts. To attack the female colleague who challenged that fact in support of the university guidelines seemed unreasonable as well. With such exacting standards, the silent votes of support raised their own concern. The silent support of Doral may mean that these faculty members did not wish to offend their senior colleagues who may be assessing *their* credentials in the near future for tenure or promotion. Perhaps the silent majority too felt they did not want to end Doral's career so abruptly. In their opinion, perhaps the dissenting colleagues took the 'letter' of the policy too seriously and should have addressed the 'spirit' of the policy and allowed Doral to ascend to Level 2 status. After all, what harm would it cause? Achievement of Level 2 status permitted the holder to chair doctoral dissertations. Either scenario shows that colleagues tended to vote more on issues less relevant to the meaning behind Level 2 instead of focusing on quality as specified in the policy.

Promoting Doral to Level 2 status with substandard credentials unknowingly sets a precedent for future department members seeking the same status. This exercise proved to be an argument for keeping Doral on the faculty rather than scrutinizing his work and voting instead to support and uphold university standards. In the future, behavior like this creates a murky, slippery slope that serves to diminish program quality. Perhaps elevating one person would not be problematic but with precedent set, it could be detrimental to long-term program quality.

Granting Doral Level 2 status also gives him a false sense of his ability and expectation as he proceeds to the tenure process the following year. His colleagues inadvertently validated his ability and ultimately led him to believe, mistakenly perhaps, that what he had accomplished at this step would be good enough for tenure and promotion to associate in a year or two. Not being privy to the meeting (we hope), the argument for awarding graduate status rested more on his family situation and real estate purchase rather than the overall quality of his work.

Another group to consider when awarding a faculty member graduate Level 2 status is the graduate student population over whose dissertations Doral may serve as chair. These students deserve quality skills and direction. His dossier indicated that he did not live up to the expectations set by the University Graduate Council. Would he take the same posture with student work? The discussion in the meeting did not revolve around this important issue either.

Luke's Early Tenure and Promotion Bid

As is typical, tenure reviews begin in the fifth or sixth year. A rising star in his field, Luke possessed enough peer-reviewed scholarly publications and stellar teaching evaluations to pursue tenure and promotion to associate in his fourth year. Luke's colleagues also considered him to be very collegial. In fact, he received high praise and remarks during his pre-tenure review process the previous year.

The university tenure document contained a provision for going up for tenure early. Luke submitted his dossier, an unprecedented move in his department. Professors with decades of seniority expressed that they were surprised and three intimated they were incensed by the candidate's actions. They felt him to be an upstart. Those with less seniority but with tenure were neither surprised by their senior colleagues nor incensed by their junior colleague's initiative.

Needless to say, the faculty discussion during Luke's P&T assessment failed to mention the quality of Luke's credentials. Instead, a few senior faculty members argued the point that the tenure document expected candidates going up in their fourth year to be 'superior.' Since no one in the meeting could apparently relate to that word, the faculty focused instead on a reason for turning down his request. They indicated that a precedent would be set in the department by his going up earlier than one would normally. These colleagues also expressed concern that Luke would be turned down at the university level review and therefore being the concerned mentors they were, they should protect him at the departmental level.

Newly tenured professors sat on the fence not wishing to upset their most senior colleagues. They either remained silent altogether or passively concurred. They did not want to hurt their own chances of promotion further down the road by bucking the old guard. The most senior colleagues were like elephants, they never forgot anything! Luke waited impatiently in his office to hear the outcome of the closed ballot vote.

Sometimes well-meaning faculty err on the side of caution. Other times they simply utilize their professional right such that their well-meaning demeanor serves as a mask to purposefully hide their obvious paternalism. In this case being paternalistic served no purpose but to damage Luke's chances for early tenure. How Luke's file would be perceived by the chair, dean, or university committee, is irrelevant to the intent of this meeting. The only discussion should have been about Luke's credentials and whether they met the stated tenure document criteria of 'superior,' despite its vagueness. They could have formulated their own conception of 'superior' and showed how closely Luke achieved it. Clearly that definition would be considered as subjective as 'collegiality' was in the first vignette. Shifting the discussion from the real reason for early tenure to other faculty-centric issues demeaned Luke and his impressive fourth-year dossier. The ensuing discussion demonstrated simply all the insecurities and dysfunctions latent in this particular department.

When you have an opportunity to secure the position of a rising star like Luke, senior faculty should focus on mentoring and supporting him rather than comparing his credentials to theirs. They could have compared Luke's credentials with recent tenured faculty who secured tenure in the normal time frame. If Luke's dossier ranked better than those of other incumbents then the faculty would be relatively confident that he achieved 'superior' status.

Having Luke on the faculty should not raise the senior faculty's insecurity level but instead raise the quality of instructional delivery, research potential, and ultimately the caliber of faculty on staff. Stars like Luke can attract graduate students and perhaps grant monies. His work has the potential to positively affect the programs being offered. Instead of focusing on what Luke may bring to the department in the future, which is one of the premises for tenure, the faculty focused on their own insecurities such that an affirmation of *his* work may affect *them* in the future. A culture of silence prevailed in this department, too. Mid-career faculty chose not to rock the boat. Even though they perhaps favored support of Luke's credentials, the focus on their own future jeopardized his.

Time was devoted to offering plausible reasons for why Luke's dossier would not be supported by others 'up the line' rather than focusing on the quality of Luke's work thus far and what it may mean to the department. The faculty's paternalistic concern for him rang empty despite their overtures to the contrary. Wanting to spare him the possibility of being turned down at the university level and thus using up one of his two chances to go up for tenure further fueled the argument. If his dossier demonstrated such high quality, he would surely achieve tenure next time on his second chance.

Unfortunately, Luke threatened the status quo. He challenged his colleagues to think differently. They operationalized their paternalism during the meeting, stating they were only looking out for his best interest. Clearly, they looked out for their own interests, not Luke's, nor the department's long-term interests. As a result of their short-sightedness, the department could lose a collegial citizen, an engaging teacher, and a consummate researcher. Perhaps it was those qualities that threatened some of Luke's senior colleagues. Ironically, if we compare this vignette with the previous vignette, setting this precedent would have created a different effect on the future of the department.

Adam's Business Contracts and Tenure

Adam was one of a kind but probably not the kind well suited to academe. His claim to fame included a consulting business through which he established a consortium of small liberal arts colleges and served as their outsourced institutional research person. He contracted with 30 colleges and charged each of them a $2000 fee to compile their annual fact books. With that money, he hired a few graduate assistants and purchased equipment to facilitate his contractual arrangement. Even with his assistants and a two-course teaching load per term, he still had little time for publishing, attending program/curriculum meetings, or devoting time to his teaching and course preparation.

Very much the gadabout, public relations schmoozer, Adam saw the campus faculty/staff health club as a place to win friends and influence high-level campus administrators. In his 'spare time,' he aligned himself with the vice president of finance, the faculty senate president, and a dean or two. When tenure and promotion time came, Adam believed that these connections would help him secure tenure, especially if his department colleagues proved to be less than generous with their votes.

When his tenure year arrived, Adam placed a very lengthy document in the department office for all his tenured colleagues to review. Once the smoke cleared and mirrors darkened, faculty saw the real spirit of the dossier. The department expected at least 10 publications in refereed journals with Adam as senior or sole author on a majority of them. Likewise, conference presentations of those papers at national and regional conferences would be the precursor to their publication. Disappointed, the faculty realized that Adam did not have 10 publications nor was he the sole author on any of them or first author on most of them. Some of them dated to before his arrival at the university. He listed in page after page each fact book he had compiled for the last five years, however, as fulfilling his service commitment. Adam's teaching evaluations and peer reviews indicated that he had made little progress in his time there. He had also struggled to maintain average teacher evaluation scores. His syllabi changed little from year to year or from course to course.

When Adam talked to faculty about his work from the time he was interviewed for the position, he indicated that the data he gathered from the liberal arts colleges would be used to further his research agenda. In fact, he boasted that there was so much data, that other faculty could have it to generate articles and presentations of their own. Several faculty members aligned themselves with Adam with the hope that this data would assist them in their own quest for tenure and/or promotion. Adam welcomed their presence as affirmation for his work and a positive tenure vote.

Imperative to securing tenure is the understanding of the requirements printed in the university tenure document. Based on his previous annual reviews, Adam received or heeded little guidance with regard to preparing for the fateful day of placing his own credentials in application for tenure. Little or no mentoring is apparent here but it could be because Adam or perhaps his colleagues did not think he would need it. Perhaps Adam ignored senior faculty attempts to help him. Perhaps his senior colleagues felt he knew enough of the process to function well enough on his own because of the data he possessed. He convinced them indirectly through his consulting job that he manipulated enough data to surely publish the expected 10 articles.

Having touted his consulting fact book business as a data gold mine to be shared by all, Adam may have believed he could circumvent the normal tenure process. However, fact book data from disparate campuses could not be used by colleagues as it would not likely parallel their existing research agendas. Oddly, the data Adam wished to give others for their research never materialized as a basis for *his own* research agenda. Clearly the fact book obligation couched in a data-for-all enterprise took away valuable time needed for improving Adam's teaching skills and/or securing peer-reviewed publications. In fact, the data-for-all promise became another way potentially to help secure a vote from the faculty members who tried to use it. They may feel beholden to Adam and thus feel guilty if they did not support him for tenure and promotion.

Commandeering the friendship of administrators who have no authority in the tenure process veered Adam further off course. Adam rationalized that these men would like him enough to go to bat for him lest he encounter a tenure snag in his department. No one informed Adam otherwise or he failed to listen if they did.

Preparing for the tenure review, Adam presented his credentials in such a way as to misrepresent his work. Consulting should not be construed as a service function. Adam received money for his consulting work; it served as a sideshow not the main event. Service is considered part of the faculty contract with the university along with research and teaching.

The fact book business took far more time than any junior faculty member has to spare. Time spent in improving teaching and writing for publication would have benefited Adam professionally at tenure time. Hiring Adam, knowing his vulnerability, placed the department in an exploitative position. On the other hand, Adam knew enough about his data to know that no one *could* use it, especially considering *he* never used it. Each side directly and indirectly deceived the other. Adam legitimized his consulting fact book business because the university housed it for him. Tenure became less important when Adam expanded his business during his pre-tenure. But that does not absolve the faculty of their shortcomings. Not only did they not mentor to Adam properly, they contemplated originally using him to seek their own publications.

Merle's Up or Out Situation

It was Merle's second year at the new university. He entered as an associate professor but without tenure. He placed his credentials in application for tenure in a mandatory up or out expectation. The P&T committee carefully reviewed his dossier. Several faculty reviewers noticed that he had spent six years at another university. They assumed that he did not get tenure there. They also noticed that his publication record was erratic with several good attempts in his first four years and then a lull that had continued since he left his previous institution. Further digging into the profile indicated that Merle may have a consulting business on the side and probably devoted much of his time to that to the exclusion of publishing. Because he was no longer teaching at a major flagship research university, he perhaps presumed publication to be less significant here.

Merle's chair presented his credentials to the P&T committee, lauding his work in all three areas. Follow-up inquiry to his chair revealed that in his two-year position he had failed to participate in university-wide faculty development activities. His teaching evaluations, which carried much weight with the new university, showed average scores. His service commitment was sparse compared to the stated guidelines in the tenure document. In order to achieve a positive tenure vote, Merle needed to be outstanding in teaching and good in research and service. Unfortunately, in no area did he shine, which rendered the department chair's strong advocacy of Merle a bit hollow. Thus, the committee voted unanimously to not award tenure or promotion to Merle.

When Merle heard the news from the dean, he hired a lawyer. Merle and his lawyer claimed that Merle should have been afforded a pre-tenure review before going up for tenure. The dean negated the faculty vote and granted him a pre-tenure review the following year. In the meantime, the dean and the faculty council chair succeeded in changing the college P&T committee composition from predominantly women to predominantly men. Of the members who voted on Merle, nine of them were replaced but two remained, including the P&T chair and the one person absent from the previous year's deliberations.

There seemed to be consistency among the faculty committee with regard to Merle's dossier in that he failed to align his work with the college's expectations for tenure and promotion. In fact, Merle's complacency with regard to participation in faculty development activities puzzled the committee. Given that he did not get tenure at his previous university, the committee may have assumed that he would do all he could to secure it here. While it is not inappropriate for faculty to have consulting businesses, his devotion to it was perhaps at the expense of his full-time position and the demands of continuing publication.

Moving from a major flagship research university to what he perceived as a smaller, less demanding institution, Merle may have presumed that he had enough to secure tenure. Perhaps his chair misled him to believe he did. The chair seemed to be out of tune with the alignment of Merle's credentials and the written tenure policy in the faculty handbook. During Merle's two years the department chair may have focused Merle's attention on other areas to Merle's detriment.

While not uncommon, the presence of lawyers in the academic mix seems to garner fear in administrators no matter how airtight the case. One could argue that Merle had his pre-tenure review at his previous institution and thus knew his standing. Because this institution fell into another Carnegie Classification, albeit research-intensive versus research-extensive, a pre-tenure review may be argued. Someone entering a university with six years of previous experience often foregoes the formality of a review and falls into the up or out category. And by Merle's own action, he failed to follow the suggested university guidelines by not availing himself of all that the new institution had to offer tenure track faculty. Without doubt, Merle's department chair failed to inform him of these expectations, which could have been addressed in a yearly performance appraisal. Mistakenly the chair believed that Merle would sail through the process given his prior record, leading one to conclude that the chair is out of touch with the tenure process and the college guidelines.

The dean bowed to pressure and opted to allow Merle the pre-tenure review, giving him another year to comply and perhaps make up for gaps in his dossier. Instead of supplying Merle with better mentoring in the interim, he decided to change the composition of the committee, a measure probably designed to help ensure that Merle would succeed once the naysayers were replaced. The emphasis rested more on constituting a committee that would approve Merle rather than on activities that would help Merle improve.

The original unanimous vote should be very telling. It should have signaled to Merle that it may be time to dig in or move on. It should tell the dean that no one on that committee regarded Merle's credentials worthy of tenure at the university. Leaving the P&T committee fairly intact with natural attrition would have produced a situation that allowed the incumbents to revisit the case and note improvements, if any, that would have produced a decision based on a clear demonstration of Merle's commitment to the university.

Francis' De Facto Tenure

His new university hired Francis with the stipulation that he would have two years to secure tenure after he was hired. Because he had 10 years at another university in a different Carnegie Classification, he would have to endure the tenure process over again. Faculty never warmed to Francis because the former dean bypassed the normal search committee hiring process to bring Francis aboard.

In his second year Francis submitted his dossier. Eligible faculty met to review his credentials. The outcome of the meeting resulted in a unanimous vote of no from the faculty and a non-supporting letter from the department chair. However, the dean supported his tenure. Unfortunately, it was not enough to sway the university committee. The chair was then tasked with informing Francis verbally of the decision and following up with an obligatory letter notifying Francis that his contract would not be renewed. Francis would have the next year to search for another position outside of the university. The chair neglected, however, to write that letter in the specified period of time so Francis received tenure through a de facto process.

We all forget to do things. However, the department chair's complacency in this matter cannot be excused as forgetfulness. The pesky question still remains as to whether the dean, knowing about de facto tenure, asked the department chair to forego writing the letter so Francis could remain. Doing so is reprehensible on both their parts but, more importantly, it allows Francis to remain in a position within a culture that never accepted him regardless of his potential to contribute to it.

Note that the vignette does not discuss Francis' teaching, research, and service but rather the fact that his condition of hiring irked his colleagues. He had achieved tenure elsewhere but not at a research institution of the caliber of the one at which he now worked so he probably did possess some of the necessary prerequisites but perhaps not all. On the flip side, perhaps the dean hired Francis to fulfill a specific void at this institution without the dean fully assessing if Francis would be a good fit with the department culture given his credentials or his potential to conduct future research.

The dean should have known his faculty well enough to know they would have been upset by this faculty appointment because he circumvented the process. However, Francis could have received mentoring in this two-year period, perhaps from the dean, the chair, or a senior faculty member, but there is no indication that he did. The entire chain of events infuses the culture with an element of suspicion that taints the roles of chair and dean to the point where both lose credibility as a result of their individual and perhaps collusive actions.

DEBRIEFING THE ROAD TO TENURE

The superhighway to tenure in research/doctoral granting universities differs from the boulevards and avenues to tenure at liberal arts and comprehensive/master's granting universities. Youn and Price (2009) illustrated this fact that nowhere is evaluation of promotion and tenure rules and expectations more evident than in comprehensive institutions where mission creep tends to be more prevalent. Many faculty members trained at major research institutions, and administrators trying to edge their institutions into research university territory raise expectations for junior faculty candidates. Standards elevated to mirror those at research institutions create angst among junior faculty applying for tenure and faculty committees taxed with reviewing those credentials. Faculty culture mirrored in committee expectations could oppose existing standards leaving the junior faculty ambivalent about their preparation as well as the outcome of the impending tenure deliberations especially when they move from one type of institution to another.

Oddly, the research universities where these four vignettes took place offer no clearer stated standards or committee expectations than what Youn and Price (2009) discussed. What appears consistent is inconsistency! However, several threads ran through the vignettes that are worth discussing. Unfortunately, evidence of manipulation, paternalism, ambiguity, and deception appeared commonplace as well.

One faculty member challenged the status quo through his early tenure application; another asked for more clarification than originally provided in a pre-tenure document. Typically, challengers of any ilk may find themselves ignored, halted, silenced, or dismissed (Fisanick, 2006; Namie & Namie, 2000; Twale & De Luca, 2008). In both instances, the P&T review committee and the candidates found themselves skeptical of the deliberation process, confused by the definition of terms used in the tenure document and the faculty interpretations of them, and minus the closure they needed to make sense of the outcomes and move forward on a corrected path. Each vignette highlighted the common complaint regarding tenure expectations printed in faculty handbooks: poor clarity with tenure document language especially with regard to espoused standards and candidate expectations (Austin & Rice, 1998; Sorcinelli, 2002). Two candidates could neither determine the university's definitions of 'collegiality' and 'superior' nor determine how the department interpreted those definitions. Faculty writing the document must provide a clear definition to assist other faculty and administration with consistency in interpretation. Euben's (2002) concern revolved around fair and consistent application of the tenure criteria over time and across all candidates in the department. In other words, standards cannot shift from pre-tenure review to tenure meeting.

Another candidate presumed that his consulting business and his affiliation with major campus players would seal his tenure bid favorably. When faculty, especially new faculty, involve themselves in auxiliary or commercial projects that interfere with their full-time faculty duties, this constitutes a conflict of commitment, in Adam's case, a major time commitment (Poskanzer, 2002; Washburn, 2005). In addition, Merle assumed that his chair and primary advocate would ensure his tenure bid. In each instance the dossiers spoke for themselves.

Even with the more exacting standards of a Graduate Council's graduate status document, neither the candidate nor the eligible voting faculty abided by them. In this instance, individual establishment of a research agenda is important but so is collaborative work. They can be mutually exclusive and counterproductive by tenure time depending upon how pre-tenure, graduate status, and annual performance appraisals align with tenure and promotion expectations. If they do not, it can confuse both candidate and committee member. This inconsistency may affect Doral's tenure despite his receiving faculty support for graduate faculty status. There is nothing to be gained by giving candidates a false sense of their ability (Austin & Rice, 1998).

The pre-tenure and graduate status reviews allow the faculty to gain insight into the junior faculty's workplace norms. During these reviews, faculty try to determine if the teaching, research, and service patterns they see now in a candidate's file will continue once the candidate obtains tenure and promotion. In other words, the process should be able to predict either a productive, long-term career, or one that may cease once tenure is awarded. In the latter case, awarding tenure would be unadvisable. What patterns the candidates show in the first five to seven years should give an indication of how they will perform once tenured. If junior faculty have ignored, manipulated, or circumvented the system now when the stakes are high and scrutiny intense, then post-tenure will likely be more of the same when the bright street light no longer shines on their credentials. Consistent and productive patterns that emerge prior to tenure, faculty believe, will likely continue post-tenure. Review committees, department heads/chairs, and deans should be cognizant of these red flags and work to modify pre-tenure candidates' paths.

Austin and Rice (1998) also mentioned the ambiguous apportionment of teaching, research, and service. For instance, what are the expectations for a candidate whose distribution is 60 percent teaching, 30 percent research, and 10 percent service compared to someone with a higher percentage in teaching but a lower percentage in research and nothing in service? Tenure committees will still expect the latter candidate to perform some campus or professional service regardless of the distribution. If the document states that teaching must be 'excellent,' then it must be excellent regardless of the distribution. If a department faculty expects that those going up for tenure have 10 articles because that is the typical amount they have seen in the last several cycles, then the committee may not view five articles as satisfactory, and therefore, not recommend tenure. However, the quality of those five articles and the journals in which they were published may be of higher quality than 10 in third-tier journals. This could sway a committee to vote in favor of the candidate but there is no guarantee following the spirit rather than the letter of the P&T document. And the ambiguity remains.

Faculty can determine if someone is 'excellent' or 'superior' in teaching or in research and also if he or she is satisfactory in the other two areas (service and either teaching or research); but tenure should not be, and typically is not, awarded to a candidate judged unsatisfactory in any one of the three areas. At research institutions, the research component must be 'good' to 'excellent' and the other two areas at least satisfactory, but if research is only satisfactory, the strength of the teaching and service may not be enough to save the candidate (Plater, 1998).

In several vignettes, faculty created their own silences in their departments moving about their individual business as if nothing was wrong or out of the ordinary (Campbell, 2000, p. 41). Lang (2005) learned during his tenure to move about his department with eyes closed and mouth shut, but he learned subsequently that "all have to participate in every single decision the department makes" (p. 54). One reason may be that making difficult decisions that end an academic career plague many senior colleagues. It renders them unable to cast a dissenting vote or even speak ill of a candidate in an open forum. Fear of one's work being judged in the future may also be a legitimate reason to remain quiet but it circumvents the openness necessary for the collegium to function properly (Franke, 2001).

Tenure can be based on "the collegial context in which colleagues share views and establish values about what constitutes good work" (Austin & Rice, 1998, p. 739). If faculty fail to engage in conversations to establish what that *is*, they will be unlikely to uphold those values and standards as a collective. In Luke's case, new faculty may not view their new culture as providing this open, collegial platform, which in turn would be communicated to them regularly and effectively. As a result, the incongruence may shutter "the commitment, motivation, and energy" new recruits bring to the department (Austin & Rice, 1998, p. 739). To not recognize and reward Luke's energy does a disservice to the collegium. By the same token, de facto tenure does a disservice to Francis as well as his colleagues.

Another theme from the vignettes revolved around committee decisions, split or unanimous. Hearn and Anderson (2002) noted that split votes signify problems that have emerged and festered for years unchecked by incumbents. Remedies, they suggested, may include "intensive socialization of junior faculty . . . thorough policy and practice on campus . . . thorough documentation and dissemination of requirements for promotion and tenure, and . . . encompassing an open discussion among senior faculty of what is to be valued and regarded by the department" (p. 525). Determining why colleagues cannot agree could reach the heart of the problem but peers must feel free to air those concerns or the problems will perpetuate. On the flip side, unanimous decisions speak volumes about the quality of the dossier but also about the committee and the departmental culture and how they regard a candidate.

Vetting processes like pre-tenure, graduate faculty status, tenure, and promotion should be devoid of politics, personal agendas, and special interests (Burgan, 2006). But each vignette offered an illustration to the contrary. We should evaluate each candidate on his or her ability to contribute to the department, personality traits that speak to being a good citizen in the department, and willingness through teaching, research, and service to contribute to the mission of the department/college/university and profession (Cahn, 1994). The process, however, tends to overlook quantified credentials in favor of faculty placing emphasis on a more informal, subjective feeling, or "good fit" (Campbell, 2000, p. 84). Lang (2005) confessed, "I don't like the idea of someone in power making judgments about me. I went into this business in part because I like my autonomy" (p. 151). Perhaps objectively applied consistency is more tolerable than subjectively applied inconsistency because the latter has the potential to include an unqualified candidate or exclude a qualified one. Plater (1998) concluded that "if tenure can be construed as the basis of citizenship through its bonds of mutual responsibility and dependence, then it can be the vehicle for a richer and more extensive set of career patterns and roles within the academic workplace" (p. 687).

One major function of the tenure deliberation rests on the dossier, that is, what is included, what is highlighted, and how the past few years appear to the P&T committee. Demonstrating that a research agenda had grown and developed and will continue to yield productive work following tenure means more than several articles haphazardly spaced or on various unrelated topics. The same practice applies to teaching. Candidates should demonstrate maturity in their teaching as evidenced by strong peer reviews, professional development, and respectable student evaluation scores. If the candidate seems marginal in either research or teaching, the committee response should be a negative vote as the candidate may become unproductive deadwood down the road if tenured (Cahn, 1994; Snyder, 2000; Stimpson, 2000).

Austin and Rice (1998) and Sorcinelli (2002) caution that what may have been favored at a candidate's entry may have shifted, especially with regard to research expectations. Administrative changes can also affect candidates. Evaluations early in a candidate's appointment may be more lenient than those done subsequently. In fact, the expectations of a newly installed chair or dean during the years before the candidate applies for tenure may differ from those given by the administrator in place when the candidate was hired. While that may not have affected anyone in these vignettes specifically, all actors in the vignettes experienced administrative turnover during their pre-tenure years, be it the chair, the dean, or both.

THE REST OF THE STORY

Dana received tenure and promotion to associate without any problem. The department raised Doral to Level 2 graduate status but he failed to get tenure the following year and, reluctantly, moved on. Luke searched for and found another job at a top research university during the year he would have gone up for tenure. The faculty deliberated on Adam's future and did not vote to award him tenure. Adam's chair and dean did not support him. When Adam called upon his health club 'buddies,' they had no power to offer assistance either. Merle had his pre-tenure review. A year later, Merle received tenure from the new committee. Francis remained at the university until retirement. The faculty was livid, the dean jumped for joy, and the department chair resigned.

BEST PRACTICES

- Every entering assistant professor receives a faculty handbook that outlines tenure and promotion guidelines. Typically, new faculty, overwhelmed by teaching duties, will give it a cursory look because that big event is five to seven years in the future. In the meantime, junior faculty will talk to everyone they can, which ensures a less than consistent response. If policy is not clear, faculty *must* ask for clarification from the chair, dean, or provost (see Lenze, 1999).

- Faculty must take advantage of faculty socialization efforts and professional development. Faculty may encourage the dean to regard his or her entering junior faculty each year as a cohort to be socialized. Successful attainment of tenure and promotion should be an informal though structured class that new faculty takes with the dean or his or her designee. In this setting the dean answers questions, offers information, provides mentoring and, above all, espouses consistency. Responses to questions are heard by all.

- Tenure dossiers should be formatted similarly and information presented in the correct places to assist P&T committees.

- New faculty must realize that only tenured faculty from their department as well as their chair and dean have the power to recommend tenure, not well-placed faculty or administrators from across campus.

- Collegiality should be a topic of discussion despite its implications in the tenure decision. Candidates must be assured they are interpreting the document correctly.

- P&T committee members and department chairs need to participate in P&T document and committee deliberation refresher seminars. These faculty members need to address interpretations relative to current department expectations. And the experience can afford the P&T committee an opportunity to review the document and decide if passages need to be amended or clarified. A by-product of this approach may do wonders for collegiality while it simultaneously diminishes confusion and ambiguity.

- Junior faculty must thoroughly know the P&T document, the process, and the standards set by the college or university. Because this information may be superficially communicated to them during the hiring process, it must be addressed as early as possible after the candidate joins the faculty. Chairs and faculty committees must evaluate junior faculty honestly, candidly, and consistently so that room for error is minimized.

- Tenure standards must be aligned with annual performance appraisal guidelines. Candidates can obtain a false sense of security if the performance appraisal rewards just one peer-reviewed published article per year but the tenure expectation is 12 peer-reviewed articles in respected journals. In this instance one article would not be rewarded but two or more would have to be accepted, as well as the quality of the journal being considered (Franke, 2001). As such, junior faculty must manage their time around what is rewarded for tenure and minimize time around what is not rewarded (Lenze, 1999).

- The university P&T document rarely includes specific examples or practical illustrations that would be helpful to pre-tenure candidates. Therefore, deans, chairs, and committee members need to be able to offer candidates specific examples of how to get from entry to tenure in the time allotted. This also implies examples for improvement. New faculty need to ask their chairs to offer specific examples in performance appraisals as well as needing to propose specific means for candidates to improve or rectify mistakes that do not currently align with the P&T document expectations. Junior faculty must look for consistency applied each year by their chair/head in performance appraisals. These periodic reviews should hold few if any surprises for the candidate at tenure time regardless of the final outcome. Finding inconsistency not only confuses the candidate, but only raises chances for legal entanglements. Because academic standards differ from legal standards, it is even more imperative that faculty P&T committees apply standards consistently and prepare candidates uniformly (Franke, 2001).

- Silverman (2004) cautioned junior faculty on how to establish collegial relationships by treating senior colleagues with respect and not boasting about personal accomplishments to them. He suggested being professional in class, at conferences, in meetings, during office hours, and with students. By the same token, he recommended junior faculty not participate in office politics or demand a preponderance of departmental resources.

- Perhaps the most consistent thread running through the vignettes is the presence of a faculty 'culture of silence' evidenced especially in the peer review meetings. In order for the collegium to function properly, faculty members must be vocal and communicate with one another civilly and honestly. For candidates to truly know where they stand, their peers must think enough of them and of the sanctity of the collegium to say what needs to be said constructively. Holding back one's views out of personal fear indicates dysfunction present in the department that needs to be addressed immediately (Harris & Hartley, 2011; Twale & De Luca, 2008).

RESOURCES

- The best resource a new faculty member can locate is his or her university faculty handbook. Familiarity with it beginning with one's first semester on campus and during the interim period cannot be overstated. Check the faculty handbook website or secure a hard copy.

- The tenure process factors prominently with the AAUP. Their website offers assistance with related issues and relevant articles on tenure (www.aaup.org/AAUP/issues/tenure/).

- Practical guides for securing tenure and promotion range from addressing issues in the process to compiling the dossier. Readers can benefit from *Tools for Dossier Success* (2010) by Burnham, Hoper, and Wright; Mallon's (2001) *Tenure on Trial*; and James Lang's (2005) *Life on the Tenure Track*. Online, I located Neal Wagner's (2006) steps for *Getting Tenure at a University* that readers may find helpful (http://cs.utsa.edu/~wagner/creative_writing/tenure.pdf). Robert Diamond (2004) offered a guide to tenure preparation in his *Preparing for Promotion, Tenure, and Annual Review*.

- Perhaps the first place new faculty may look when they enter a new position is to Eley et al.'s (2012) *Becoming a Successful Early Career Researcher* and also Robert Boice's (1990) *Professors as Writers*, Joseph Moxley's (1992) *Publish, Don't Perish* or Drake and Jones' (1997) *Writing Your Way to Success*. All authored texts assist faculty with the basics of scholarly writing and publishing.

Chapter 7
Conferencing and Publishing

INTRODUCTION

Not only does the road to tenure include conference presentation and article publication, but yearly merit pay and promotion to full professor also require a professor to continue to generate presentations and publications. Ironically, little scholarly research, presentation, or publication exists on these essential academic functions. Boyer (1990) brought the issue of expanding acceptable forms of publishing and scholarship to the forefront with his *Scholarship Reconsidered*. His pivotal work spawned thousands of articles and perhaps an equal number of discussions at faculty meetings and conferences.

Many authors penned guides to writing technically and facilitating book and article publication; however, studies on faculty perceptions of researching, conferencing as it relates to professional development, the effects of rejection on their subsequent publication, or ethical issues related to journal writing, submission, and contributions and authorship remain sparse in the scholarly literature. Significant scholarship exists on the merits of faculty research collaboration, conference networking, and mentorship as effective means of encouraging new faculty presentation and publication but not the more personal aspects of conferencing and publishing.

The following vignettes depict situations that stem from the lack of strong publication and conference guidelines in faculty departments due in part to the absence of similar information presented to new faculty and doctoral students preparing for academic careers in professional fields. Ironically, research universities grant tenure and rank on successful attempts in publication and presentation, but often new faculty must determine on their own how best to accomplish that.

John, Joe, and Austin Manipulate the System

Having retired as a school superintendent, John thought his work credentials spoke for themselves so he had done little research and writing during his first three years in his new academic position. As crunch time approached and he needed publications and presentations to present for his pre-tenure review, he sought advice from a senior colleague, Tim, who had done little publishing himself. Tim suggested that John simply change the title of his last presentation and submit it to another professional conference. John felt he had a new lease on life.

During his years before tenure review, Joe coasted along taking flying lessons, enjoying his grandchildren, and traveling to many conferences with his spouse, also an academic. But, he rarely presented any research. Joe's wife worked in an unrelated department as a tenured faculty member in another university. When the faculty reviewed Joe's dossier for graduate faculty status, his articles featured him as second, third, or fourth author. Joe's wife appeared as first author on one of them and second and third author on the other two. Although the articles appeared in second-tier scholarly journals, none were in Joe's area.

Austin expected to take an early retirement but following the unexpected death of his wife, he decided to stay on the faculty. However, in anticipation of retirement, he failed to publish any articles the previous two years and needed at least one to be reappointed to the graduate faculty in order to chair several dissertations he still had in the queue. He overheard a conversation between two of his younger colleagues who were completing an empirical research project. Austin had worked with each of them in the past. He asked if they would put his name on their manuscript if he edited the piece for them before they sent it off to a journal.

Perhaps department chairs/heads *presume* that new faculty know how to write and submit manuscripts for conference presentation or journal review. Getting their research agenda on track as well as knowing how to properly format a conference proposal or submit an article for publication seems to be information that administrators should convey to their new faculty recruits and that dissertation chairs may share with their students. Subtleties such as submitting the same proposal/article to two different conferences, submitting a published article to a conference for presentation, adding one's name to an article that one did not write but only edited, and/or tacking one's name to a spouse's work should be discussed with new faculty. Obviously, lack of knowledge or lack of integrity explained Tim suggesting that John resubmit his paper under a different title, and Joe's spouse and Austin's colleagues allowing their names to appear on works they did not do. On the other hand, the competition to acquire slots at conference proceedings, inclusion in prestigious journals, and/or tenure in a department may cause new faculty to accomplish goals by whatever means possible in the absence of consistent information. While they may presume these acts are of marginal integrity, faculty may truly not know the rules of the game and resort or fall prey to the tricks of the trade instead.

If at First You Don't Succeed, Yell at the Editor

As a newly appointed associate provost, Mary Kay sprouted her peacock feathers and danced a victory lap. While most administrators tended to have little time to publish, she set time aside to continue her research agenda. Mary Kay had just finished an article of which she was quite proud. Typically, faculty select an appropriate journal to which to send their manuscript and write a cover letter highlighting its alignment with that journal in hopes that the peer reviewers and editor will look favorably upon their manuscript.

Normally Mary Kay spoke with the editors personally in order to laud the contents of her article. She tended to select initially only top-tier journals as outlets for her scholarship. Even though she schmoozed one editor of a particularly prestigious journal before she submitted her manuscript, she could hardly contain herself when her rejection letter appeared in her mailbox weeks later. Acceptance rate for this journal, at only 10 percent, should have prepared her for possible rejection, but then again Mary Kay never thought that her work would fall outside of that percentage point. Furious, Mary Kay phoned the editor again to express her disappointment and perhaps plead with her to reconsider. The editor listened to her 10-minute rant, name calling, and uncivil display before terminating the conversation.

Senior faculty members and administrators should know better than to prime the pump in order to get published. While it is perfectly acceptable to contact an editor by phone or email to discern if one's manuscript topic would be one that would be of interest to the readership, the inquiry should not be construed as a strategic move to increase one's chances for publication.

At one time or another, every faculty member has received a rejection letter from a scholarly journal. Good journal editors use reviewers' comments to offer suggestions to assist the author. That letter from the editor should be written to ease the pain of rejection and support the author rather than engender feelings of animosity or disdain that affect their writing subsequent publishable works. By the same token, civility dictates that authors receive rejections with grace, realize the reviewers dislike the piece, not them, and that the article needs work before it is resubmitted to another journal. What caused Mary Kay to disrespect the journal editor remains a mystery, but ego, position, and desire to be published in a premier journal may surely have played a role. Regardless, her behavior was inexcusable.

Articles should be written for a particular journal such that it captures the interest of the readership, falls within the confines of the space allotted, follows empirical research preferences, and adheres to the expectations set forth by the journal's board. The tendency to seek inclusion in prestigious, top tier journals is laudable, but it may be unrealistic for early career faculty who publish infrequently or have no mentors to critique drafts of their work. Carefully selecting the journal, graciously accepting the outcome, and then reading reviewers' comments to help enhance their work tends to create more success than Mary Kay attained. Had she contacted the editor to discuss how she might have improved the piece and/or thanked the editor for the comments in the face of rejection, Mary Kay would have preserved her professional reputation rather than tarnished it. Perhaps her subsequent work on another topic would have met the expectations of this top tier journal.

Invisible Colleagues at the Conference

Everyone in the department looked forward to their national professional conference each fall. So did the departmental administrative assistants because the entire faculty, and the chair would be gone all week. Some faculty presented papers while some served as discussants or did both. Ronda was excited because her family lived in the conference destination city.

The department paid for banquet tickets for all faculty members this year. Even the dean attended. Everyone presented at least one paper or served as a discussant except for Ronda and Danny. Tongues wagged when it became conspicuous that Ronda's seat at the banquet table remained empty. Danny loved to play golf, chat with old friends, and dine at fine establishments when at conferences so he missed the event as well. No one saw Ronda or Danny attend any of the sessions either. In fact, since the trip in from the airport, no one had talked to or seen Ronda. When Ronda and Danny returned to their offices, they submitted their travel vouchers along with their colleagues.

Some reasons to patronize local, regional, and national conferences include: furthering the profession by introducing the latest cutting-edge research to the field for colleague critique before submitting it to a journal; discussing the future direction of the profession; introducing and nurturing new entrants into the profession; and positioning one's university as a major player in research venues. In addition, conferences market themselves as furthering professional development and colleague networking and as offering leadership opportunities for colleagues to fulfill professional service obligations. Years ago academic departments provided ample travel money for faculty to pursue these opportunities in enjoyable locations across the country. As budgets tightened, travel monies declined and faculty gradually either attended fewer conferences per year or opted to spend their own money to further their careers.

This particular department splurged in order for all members to attend the big banquet. Ronda and Danny were obligated to attend. Attending some of the sessions to further their professional development would not be out of the question, especially considering the fact they were neither presenters nor discussants. The presence of the dean and the department chair should have signaled to them the importance of the conference and their participation in it. Professional organizations, especially the smaller regional ones, struggle to survive amid system-wide budget cuts coupled with the rising costs of hotel and food service. Not patronizing conferences places them in jeopardy of extinction. They serve a vital mission to their respective professions and disciplines that in their absence would surely create a major void. Ronda and Danny seem to have lost sight of the vital role an association plays, not to mention their attendance.

DEBRIEFING CONFERENCING AND PUBLISHING

Blasycyznski, Scott, and Green (2009) noted that conference attendance positively correlates with faculty vitality with regard to scholarly publication. In other words, if vetted through a peer-review process with concomitant feedback offered, a conference presentation tends to be something worth submitting to a scholarly or practitioner journal. Not all presentations will result in publications; however, a CV with myriad conference papers but only a few publications indicates a problem that should be detected by chairs during annual performance appraisals.

By contrast, multiple and sole authorships indicate well-rounded academics who satisfy norms for research collaboration as well as fulfilling the commitment to a coherent research agenda. Spouses collaborating on publications could have negative repercussions for either party. Because the topic of the articles appeared to be out of Joe's area of expertise, it may lead peers voting on his status to conclude that his wife did the work and simply added his name. Such practices may be collaborative but these articles fell outside of his research agenda. Intellectual autonomy needs to be made clear to peers, and in this instance, it was not (Creamer, 2006).

Similar to a Darwinist natural selection process, faculty put forth effort to see their scholarship published in prestigious journals (Blasycyznski et al., 2009; Bray & Major, 2012). It would not be unusual for faculty like Mary Kay to submit to these journals first but it may be counterproductive for many new faculty who need more confidence in their writing ability. Valle and Schultz (2011) found that senior faculty tended to publish in top-tier journals for several reasons: (a) in order to establish a research agenda; (b) knowledge of their readership; (c) supported by doctoral students; (d) likely to receive incentives or rewards to publish; and (e) it honed their ability to write over their career. Junior faculty may not be privy to these at entry but must gradually build up capital over time. In other words, senior faculty, especially those in research institutions, accumulate and use to their advantage the social, cultural, and political capital needed for researching, presenting, and publishing. This same study found a positive correlation between faculty productivity in top-tier outlets and journal editorial board membership.

Burke and James (2010) questioned the inter-rater reliability of peer review. They pondered factors that influence ratings of peers' research performance, a factor that may preoccupy tenure committees. They determined that peers' assessments indicated they favored objective rather than subjective or political factors when rendering a decision of accept or reject. This should be good news to those submitting manuscripts in that the process espouses fairness and rejections are more common than acceptances.

Above all, faculty need to pay close attention to publishing norms in their department/college as well in their field/discipline (Minton, Fernando, & Ray, 2008). They must not only be cognizant of how much they need to publish but also where. Specifically, colleagues may establish a set number of peer-reviewed articles with expectations for them to be in specific journals or in the top tiers. Journals may be selective of what types of empirical research they will accept as representative of what the field/discipline regards as significant (Blasycyznski et al., 2009). New faculty need to also be aware of the audience for which they write and the value placed on that in the department/college. For instance, journals read by practitioners may not be a suitable outlet for one's research and may not be valued by tenure committees.

THE REST OF THE STORY

John did as his mentor Tim suggested. By tenure time, however, the P&T committee realized that John's presentations had a peculiar similarity. The faculty saw through Joe and he failed to achieve graduate faculty status and departed at the end of the semester for non-academic pursuits. Austin's colleagues regrettably put his name on their paper out of deference to his senior status and personal loss. Mary Kay learned little from her encounter with the journal editor and continued to push her agenda on the next unsuspecting editor. Ronda decided to leave the institution before her tenure time and take a position outside academe. Danny retired shortly after this conference. Neither the dean, the chair, nor the attending faculty inquired of or admonished Ronda or Danny for their conference faux pas.

BEST PRACTICES

Conferencing and publishing remains an area that needs to be mined in the scholarly literature. Aspects also need to be addressed in professional development seminars.

CONFERENCING AND PUBLISHING

- If new faculty did not have strong graduate school mentors who published prolifically or received degrees from institutions other than Research Intensive/Extensive, then stronger mentoring needs to exist for these faculty novices. Indeed, the earlier concept of pushing for a new faculty cohort class could cover the expectation for conference protocol in depth and then concentrate on translating presentations into publications by selecting the best scholarly outlet.

- The annual performance appraisal meeting should also be a time to encourage faculty to seek developmental options on how to convert a presentation to a manuscript. New faculty may need to ask their chair about their best hope for publication. They need to realize it lies in peer-reviewed presentations. A lopsided CV consisting of many presentations and few publications indicates faculty resisting writing for publication. Junior faculty need to be told by chairs or seek professional development opportunities on their own.

- Graduate department faculty should illuminate their doctoral students preparing for academic careers on conference presentation and journal publication protocol. Conferences typically include a session or two on getting published. PhD candidates and junior faculty should attend. Faculty need to shepherd their PhD students to conferences.

RESOURCES

- Numerous books exist to assist doctoral students and new faculty. Pat Thomson and Barbara Kamla's (2012) *Writing for Peer Reviewed Journals* offers a perspective on successful writing for publication. Patricia Goodson (2013) adds another practical approach with her book, *Becoming an Academic Writer*.

- For faculty sitting on P&T committees and judging colleagues' work, several library reference texts offer assistance: *Cabell's Directory of Publishing*, which separates disciplinary journals into several guides; *Thomson Reuters Web of Knowledge* (http://thomsonreuters.com/products_services/science/science_products/a-z/isi_web_of_knowledge/); *Journal Citation Reports*; and the *Google Scholar Search Hirsch Index* (http://code.google.com/p/citations-gadget/). Readers must be cautioned that not all journals in which articles are published are referenced in these resources but it gives committee members and faculty a comparative indication of scholarly work (Hodge & Lacasse, 2011).

Chapter 8
Campus Service and Institutional Citizenship

INTRODUCTION

While teaching and research roles are easy to define, service functions tend to be broader. They span serving on departmental, college, and university committees that include candidate searches, faculty senate, human subjects, tenure and promotion, curriculum, budget, student affairs, academic honesty, discipline, grievance, and even parking. Professional service comprises reading conference and grant proposals, peer-reviewing articles or serving as editor of a journal, and assuming various roles in a professional association, such as conference planning.

Different types of service may be restricted by rank and tenure while others may require networking to secure appointment. Campuses may post a call for faculty interested in serving on committees with upcoming vacancies. Some committee service is ad hoc, determined by specific term, or regulated ex officio by virtue of holding another position. Often the important criterion for serving on committees is not on what one serves but on how many or how much time service consumes to the detriment of teaching and research.

Service involvement may parallel a faculty member's field or discipline in such a way as to open a door for research or teaching opportunities. Combining one's service appointments with opportunities to research and publish makes the task less an obligation and more of a practical, rewarding experience (Boyer, 1990). Service commitments could allow the faculty member to explore unknown aspects of the university. Appointments facilitate networking with other colleagues across campus that could lead to collaborative research opportunities. Fulfilling certain functions like faculty senate or P&T committee permit professors to participate in governance, direct the course of the university curriculum, recommend that the trustees extend permanent employment to colleagues, or introduce new policies that protect academic freedom. Outreach opportunities permit faculty to give back to their community through their research and teaching.

By the same token, service obligations can be time-consuming, political quagmires that can stall academic policy and progress as well as derail individual careers. Faculty assumes service roles to the detriment of their other duties only to discover that serving on committees may not be rewarded at tenure time. In Chapter 2, Nancy learned that her chairing the search committee to hire five new colleagues could have placed her tenure in jeopardy. Not only would the task consume her valuable time needed to produce the scholarship the department valued and rewarded, but as an untenured faculty member, she could have found herself at odds with the tenured faculty members who would be casting a vote on her in the near future.

The following case vignettes highlight issues of the second variety with the hope that new faculty can avoid the pitfalls inherent in campus service. For tenured faculty service obligations can be rewarding and collegial but not necessarily less political or contentious.

The Graduate Council's Newest Member

Beverly expressed professional gratitude at having been appointed to the university's Graduate Council. Without receiving guidelines about the purpose of this committee, she could only speculate on what she would be expected to do. She knew she would be voting on faculty from across the campus on their appointment to graduate faculty. In addition, requests from departments for new courses or significant changes to existing ones would need to be approved.

During the first meeting, the council always voted on graduate level status for new applicants. Weeks ago Beverly received a packet containing CVs of colleagues from across the campus on whom she would be voting. She noted the distinct differences in their credentials. But all were seeking the same status. In the meeting discussion that ensued, Beverly expressed her observations. Other members of the committee looked at Beverly in bewilderment. The council chair dismissed her concerns by stating that if everyone despite their credentials does not get appointed to graduate level status, they would not be able to teach the graduate courses they currently oversee. Everyone went along with the statement and voted to raise the status of all candidates regardless of how closely they met the written requirements.

Committee members forget that new members like Beverly may come to the post with enthusiasm, not realizing the prevailing tenor or culture of this council. As a result, the dissonance Beverly encountered between her work ethic and that of the council left her dumbfounded, too. On the other hand, she did not realize how this committee conducted their business and they may have legitimate reasons or rationale for what they did and why they did it that way. In retrospect Beverly probably should have listened more than she spoke in order to gain perspective as well as observe the council's inner workings. She needed to observe the machine in action to see who operated it, who oiled it, and who repaired it. In the council's eyes, Beverly attempted to throw a wrench into the machine even though she thought her perspective improved it. The committee vote indicated how *they* intended to keep the machine running.

The Promotion and Tenure Committee

Each year the composition of the college P&T committee varied as people entered new terms and others cycled off. However, the chair of the committee seemed to remain from year to year. In fact, Ben prided himself on being the most senior member of the committee. He informed the others that he should be chair again this year. He also told the committee that they need not bother with appointing a secretary from among the faculty committee members as per the by-laws as he would volunteer his personal secretary for the job. Ben agreed that he would write whatever letters needed to be written as they would be regarded as confidential and, thus, his secretary should not do that. Lois reluctantly accepted Ben's terms as she was new to this committee though a seasoned veteran of P&T committees at a previous university. Lois had not yet read the by-laws.

When her second year on the committee began, Lois prepared herself for the first fall meeting. She read the by-laws beforehand and attended this meeting prepared to engage in the discussion. Once again Ben insisted he be chair this year even though he informed the group that he would miss several meetings given his very busy schedule. Another committee member suggested that Ben not be chair, but instead nominated Lois. The committee, except Ben, seemed pleased with the change. Meeting adjourned.

Promptly, Ben stomped into the dean's office to tell him what had happened. When Lois answered the knock on her office door, she was surprised to see the dean. He informed Lois that the appointment for P&T chair is for three years and, therefore, Ben had every right to it despite his busy schedule. Therefore, she could not be chair. Lois countered with the fact that, last year, Ben told the committee, mostly all new members, that the member with seniority must be chair. As per the by-laws that is not true, she added, and thus, he had taken advantage of the situation the year before. The dean mentioned that Ben had called another meeting of the committee for tomorrow to discuss this development.

Lois attended the meeting the following day. Proudly, Ben announced his re-enthronement to the chair position as per the dean's intervention. He then informed everyone present that his secretary would continue as recording secretary this year. With the by-laws in hand, Lois interrupted to read that the secretary to the committee must be a faculty member on the committee. She gazed at Ben and said, "if you want to abide by the policy, that's fine, but you have to abide by the whole policy, not just the parts that favor you." The committee member who nominated Lois the previous day jumped up and gleefully agreed to be the new secretary. Problem solved. Meeting adjourned.

When Lois talked with her closest colleague later that day to recount the course of events, her colleague informed her that she may have seemingly won the battle but the war Ben privately declared would rage on until Ben declared his victory over Lois. Beware of landmines planted in your path, she warned.

Committee work should embody collegiality in action. Unfortunately, Lois and Ben set a tone that prevented it from happening. Locking horns for whatever reason created a contentious environment for the whole committee. Regardless of whether one person wishes to exert power over another or one person desires to follow the rules and another does not, each situation indicates that one party will be at odds with the other. Regardless of how the dean felt about the situation, he acted in accordance with the rules that dictated how that committee wished to be governed *now*. Perhaps a savvy Lois would have challenged Ben the previous year to prevent his rise to chair but her limited knowledge of the by-laws benefited Ben. Receiving/Reading the by-laws for committee members should be done beforehand. Ignorance of them by committee members silently allowed Ben to manipulate matters to his desired advantage. Once Ben established the rules the way he desired, a culture began to form that then became difficult for Lois to fathom *or* change. Although she made valiant attempts to follow the by-laws once she read them, her actions derailed any collegiality that previously existed and triggered a competition between her and Ben. Even though she had the by-laws on her side per se the second year, Ben's power and the dean's authority could not be penetrated. She only realized that following her consultation with a revered colleague and by then the damage was done.

I Never Said That!

The Program Coordinators Committee met once per month. Doug had the habit of making policy or changing policy to suit his purposes. Then, if a student or faculty member petitioned the committee and it challenged his policy, he would argue against the policy and ask the committee to revise it rather than acknowledge his short-sightedness. On one occasion, Connie recalled to Doug that he authored the policy in question. Doug disagreed. Other members of the committee either sat contently on the fence or hinted that perhaps Connie may be right. But Doug insisted that he did not pen that particular policy. As he contemplated the new wording for the policy, he asked Art, the chair, to document his dictations. Art complied. Several months later the same thing happened again. Doug denied authorship, Connie challenged, Art suffered temporary memory loss, Doug dictated, and once again Art documented.

Some personalities overshadow others on committees. Again the idea to work collegially cannot occur when one personality dominates. In order for that personality to dictate, others on the committee must allow it to happen. Collegial relations suffer when people dominate and others challenge in ways that are not related to the issue but rather to the functioning of the committee. They argued over who penned the policy rather than trying to make better articulation of the policy itself the object of their focus. Doug tended to dominate the discussions and usurp the authority of the chair. By their ambivalence, remaining members failed to support Art or Connie and thus allowed the culture Doug created to prevail. Art should be the first to set the record straight and devise a new way to move the discussions to policy revision in ways that prevent Doug from changing his mind in precarious situations. In addition, Art, along with the rest of the silent majority, needs to address working collegially once Doug's dominance diminishes.

Get with the Program

Melissa decided her first year on this committee would be best served if she listened more than she spoke. She wanted to get the lay of the land, and understand the culture and the personalities of the players before she participated totally. Experience told her to be cautious.

By contrast, Drew expected Melissa to take the lead even though he served in the capacity of chair. However, he accepted her silent role in the meetings at first because she delivered when it came to producing academic reports. During the fall of her second year on the committee, Drew lost his temper and called Melissa into his office after a meeting. He told Melissa she was not doing her job and her silence was clearly a plot to undermine his role as committee chair. Drew said that she never produced agenda items for the meetings, which proved that she simply coasted along in her role.

Surprised and incensed at his assessment, Melissa spent that afternoon devising 25 agenda items that would surely keep meetings going for a couple of years. Melissa emailed Drew her list along with a thank you for helping to light a fire under her and comments expressing a hope that the committee would be able to take the time to address some of her agenda items during the year ahead.

It appears that neither Drew nor Melissa possessed a clear definition of their respective roles on the committee. As a result, the tension between the two prevented a collegial relationship. Drew's reaction to Melissa's silence resulted in an equal and opposite reaction from Melissa in response to Drew's assessment of her work. Name calling and retaliation seldom advance the enterprise.

Melissa's early silence should not be construed as unusual. She played that correctly as she studied the culture and the operatives on the committee and processed the culture before she acted. Drew interpreted her silence differently, which may or may not have been due to his personality as well as his expectations for her role on the committee. Melissa knew nothing of Doug's expectations for her until Doug erupted. While her 25 agenda items indicated her willingness to be a team player and comply with Doug's wishes, she postured with her email response that she tempered with a sarcastic, tongue-in-cheek 'thank you.' Neither party acted like peers, colleagues, or adults.

Melissa and Doug needed to talk long before the fall of her second year. If Melissa's silence troubled Doug personally and professionally then he needed to make the first move. She assumed she performed adequately while he did not. A simple chat over coffee may have diffused the situation. An introductory letter of expectations may have been appropriate. Her reaction, while demonstrating she had the capacity to generate agenda items and perform her service duties, came across as retaliatory rather than collegial. This proved to be another time they needed to air their concerns to further a collegial relationship.

DEBRIEFING CAMPUS SERVICE AND INSTITUTIONAL CITIZENSHIP

Performing campus service simply to fulfill obligations or tenure expectations delivers a different message than caring about fulfilling the institutional mission through service, establishing a loyalty to the institution, or contributing to the smooth governing of the university. These varying motivations indicate that while serving is a time-honored tenet of higher education, faculty also espouse adherence to the time-consuming expectation of intellectual pursuits that result in tenure (Berberet, 1999) and service may not be the primary one.

Twale and Shannon (1996) addressed service involvement, rewards for service, and the need to shield new faculty. They found that women preferred professional service to campus service because departmental and college service may create tense situations at tenure time. This could have factored prominently with any of the women in the vignettes.

Furthermore, Berberet (1999) contended that "the service dimension of faculty roles remains vaguely defined, unevenly distributed, poorly rewarded, and intellectually disconnected from teaching and research" (p. 32). Each vignette illustrated these sentiments and placed each committee's ability to be collegial in jeopardy. Lang's (2005) service experience showed him that service guidelines remain non-existent, and guidance from colleagues and department chairs can be sporadic, inconsistent, or non-existent. Left up to individual choices, new faculty may select too much or devote more time and energy to service than they should (Koblinsky et al., 2006). Strong commitments to a service function will never compensate for average performance in the classroom or in scholarly publications. As a result, Baez (2000) argued that the service function, although relegated to a negligible position, supports university missions and thus should be accorded greater agency. The vignettes illustrate that faculty service requires not only time but psychic energy when it threatens collegiality.

In their study, Demb and Wade (2012) learned that the majority of participants engaged in various outreach-type activities. Ironically participation paralleled the university mission but from a cost–benefit perspective proved time-consuming for faculty as it related to tenure. The authors concluded that large research universities that support decentralized "department-level culture, policies, and procedures that affect [time] allocation and tenure have the greatest impact on faculty" (p. 358). How faculty operationalizes the service function varies widely by professor.

THE REST OF THE STORY

Beverly learned the culture of the Graduate Council and worked well within it for the remainder of her term. Lois and her colleague who served as secretary of the committee served out their terms but neither were nominated to serve a second term even though it was sanctioned in the by-laws. Tired of having to take the revisions dictated by Doug, Art told Connie privately that the next time he would make Doug write the information so it would be in his *own* handwriting. Then, there would be no mistaking who suggested the policy revision. Connie suggested that Art laminate the information just in case. Drew addressed few if any of the items Melissa suggested in her 25-item agenda list. In fact, meetings went to every other month. In the fall a new faculty member came on board the committee. Further threatened, Drew called no meetings at all that semester. The dean removed Drew from his directorship. Melissa worked successfully with the director who replaced Drew.

BEST PRACTICES

- Faculty need to select service activities that mesh with their research agenda. For instance, service activities can frame research agendas that address critical issues and barriers related to social change or social justice (Baez, 2000; Boyer, 1990). Tenure and promotion committees may examine a dossier from the standpoint of how well faculty integrate teaching, research, and service rather than just look at the elements of the trinity separately (Baez, 2000).

- Because service or committee work signify ways in which faculty demonstrate collegiality, faculty must use these opportunities to display good institutional citizenship toward colleagues and avoid posturing and contentious encounters.

- While tending to focus most on research, doctoral program curriculums, advisors, and dissertation chairs often overlook the importance of preparing candidates for academic teaching and service roles. Incorporating information and opportunities related to service and professional involvement as well as role-modeling good institutional citizenship to doctoral students should not only provide students with paths to follow but also prepare them to fulfill their future civic responsibilities on and off campus (Berberet, 1999).

- Because research and relevant literature remain sparse on the faculty service function, new faculty may learn about service by asking faculty senate presidents and administrators in the provost's office about university service, the dean about college service, and the department chair about departmental service.

- Conferences should provide information about involvement in professional service.

- Ask colleagues and mentors involved in campus and professional service to supply information about their service and the path to seeking various types of appointments.

RESOURCES

- To understand the expectations for service with regard to tenure and promotion read the faculty handbook and discuss the extent of involvement with your chair.

Chapter 9
Faculty and Administrator Relationships

INTRODUCTION

Often professors who step from their tenured ranks into administrative appointments tend to be regarded as alien beings by the faculty colleagues they left behind. They still work in the same academic culture but they now view it from different perspectives and thus develop different realities about what it should be and what direction it should take. Faculty assumes department head/chair and dean positions for varying reasons ranging from financial gain to duty to one's institution. Unfortunately, many experience difficulty transitioning to their new role while still maintaining affinity for their previous role (Carroll & Wolverton, 2004). Department *heads*, while answering to the dean at whose pleasure they serve, differ from department *chairs* who must liaise between department and dean while being "responsible for and answerable to faculty colleagues" (Hecht, 2004, p. 40). Thus, the career move from academic to academic leader and/or manager tends to confound chairs/heads. The role shift takes time either in leader preparation or management skill development as well as role socialization and on-the-job training (Gmelch, 2004). The vignettes in this chapter illustrate the difficulty of these roles and responsibilities following transition.

Department Chair Takes Advantage of New Post

Ruth and Tyanne worked on a departmental application for an entire semester in order to secure program membership on a very prestigious professional board. They gathered data, responded to all questions asked by the board, scheduled and supervised the on-campus visit, and prepared the final document. As untenured faculty, they received neither course release nor financial compensation. Entrance onto the board appeared to be its own reward.

When the confirmatory letter came that spring, Ruth, Tyanne, the chair, and the dean celebrated with the rest of their faculty colleagues. The chair anticipated asking Ruth to serve as the school's representative on the board but the chair vacated her position that summer. Ruth and Tyanne, along with the dean and newly elevated chair, Mickey, would be attending the conference. Even the dean suggested that Ruth's and Tyanne's travel expenses should be covered through their departmental travel fund to compensate them for their stellar efforts.

Anticipating the fall conference at a western resort, Ruth and Tyanne made their plane and hotel reservations. Ruth looked forward to representing the school on the board but wondered why she never received any information to that effect. A call to the board's chair confirmed that Mickey appointed himself as the representative even though this was not his area of expertise. Ruth and Tyanne also learned that Mickey spent the allotted money on his own travel needs and there was nothing left to offset the cost of theirs.

Appealing to the dean, Ruth and Tyanne pleaded that Mickey used his authority to make the self-appointment and used all the previously promised travel money. Mickey argued to the dean that he has every right to do so as neither Ruth nor Tyanne had tenure. While the dean did not remove Mickey as board rep, he assured Ruth she would sit there next year and that she and Tyanne would be funded fully from the dean's discretionary travel monies.

Changes in administration often leave colleagues in the lurch, especially following informal promises made by their predecessor. Perhaps the exiting chair did not inform the dean that Ruth was poised and groomed to be the school's new representative, or that Ruth and Tyanne would be rewarded for their work by receiving travel money from the department. The fact that Mickey knew little of the professional organization or its expectations for representation, taught in areas outside the organization's realm, did little scholarly publishing, or made no conference presentations in the past decade could have signaled to the former chair and dean that he would probably not be interested in going to the organization's annual meeting. Given the organization's board, representatives consisted of prolific researchers and well-known former administrators from across the country. Mickey had neither the background nor the reputation to thrive in their environment. Ruth possessed the grit, the respect, *and* the credentials to succeed in that environment as well as bringing accolades to the department and program for her efforts.

Mickey justified using the travel money as school representative to the organization's board, which the dean could not dispute. However, the dean needed to inform Mickey when he took office that Ruth would be the school's representative to the board, assuming the dean knew that. The former chair may not have informed the dean of her anticipated appointment or rationale. Their unfortunate oversight cost Ruth and the department more than the travel money.

Because of Ruth's and Tyanne's untenured status, they found themselves in precarious positions. First, taking on the task of preparing the document took away time from their research, teaching, and publishing. Second, agreeing to take on the role of school representative could have likewise compromised Ruth's time. Third, participating in the battle over the travel funds with the chair who failed to recognize his professional shortcomings or reward those of his faculty may have affected their relationship with him come tenure time. Fourth, arguing that Ruth rather than Mickey should be the representative and hoping to reverse that decision with the dean was pointless. While Mickey should not have been the self-proclaimed representative and should have recognized Ruth's abilities, Ruth and Tyanne assumed their challenge would dethrone Mickey. Once Mickey made his decision and began to set it in stone, the dean felt obliged to uphold it even when he realized it was a poor one. Funding their trips became their consolation prize. The dean upheld this prior administrative decision in order to recognize good work from junior faculty; Mickey did not. However, the dean chose wisely to let the situation ride this year and implement change next year.

Christine's Yearly Performance Appraisal

A seasoned associate professor, Christine dreaded this year's performance appraisal meeting with her department head, Dick. They had a falling out a few months ago. The tenured faculty supported Christine and took a no-confidence vote on the department head. Dick circled the wagons and held his ground with the support of the dean.

Because of the animosity that had developed, Christine decided to hide a tape recorder in her purse before she entered the performance appraisal meeting. She checked with a local attorney, and such activity was legal in her state. As the tape rolled, Christine and Dick talked about her teaching, research, and service. Nothing on the tape indicated anything untoward or unprofessional. In fact, the meeting proceeded better than she originally thought it would.

As is the case following each performance appraisal, the department head chronicles the meeting, and then sends a copy to the faculty member to sign to verify their conversation. While the sections on teaching, research, and service proved accurate, Dick added a fourth section summarizing the reason for their falling out. When Christine read that, she refused to sign the appraisal form and promptly sent it back to Dick.

Meanwhile, Christine made a phone call to her campus AAUP representative, Alan. During their meeting, Christine played the tape and Alan verified that what she and Dick discussed there appeared in the performance appraisal. However, nowhere on the tape did he hear the contents of the final paragraph. He indicated that the AAUP supported her case because she has valid, legal documentation. As per AAUP policy, Alan scheduled a meeting between Christine and Dick with Alan presiding to discuss the reasons for adding the final paragraph to the performance appraisal without formally discussing its content in their original meeting.

Alan noticed that Dick visibly shook during the meeting, and stumbled over his words. But Dick decided not to remove the paragraph in question from the appraisal. Alan could not recall presiding over such a case or dealing with a more aloof department head than Dick. Christine never signed her performance appraisal that year.

No faculty/department head relationship should evolve to the point that a faculty member feels the need to carry a hidden recording device in order to 'catch' a colleague. Without a tape recorder, however, Christine would not have had a clear case to take to the AAUP. It would have become a he said/she said situation. Fortunately the AAUP chapter on campus provided faculty with the support that Alan offered Christine even though Christine was not a member of this university chapter. In the meeting, Alan reminded Dick that performance appraisal guidelines necessitate that only the conversation spoken in the meeting can appear in the final document. To amend it with personal information unrelated to merit expectations seemed to further destroy the spirit of collegiality.

First Female Dean

When the founding dean retired from his position after 20 years, a search identified internal and external candidates. Extensive work needed to be done in the college as the last few years saw some complacency occurring within the departments, among staff and faculty personnel, and in various programs. Hiring from outside would supply the fresh perspective the college needed. The search committee offered the position to a former dean and female candidate, Gerri. Her most significant challenges came not from all that needed to be addressed but more from the internal male candidate, Gene, who did not get the position he coveted and that he assumed naturally would be his.

Very tenacious, Gerri cleaned house, restored integrity, and shored financial leaks by eliminating unproductive programs and personnel. But her plan contradicted her rival's and his staunch allies. She discovered fraud in one department for which she removed the chair and replaced him with a man of proven leadership skill, integrity, and a fine work ethic. She eliminated programs not germane to the mission of the college.

Gerri's leadership skill and agenda became evident and the college benefited from her efforts. Allies of Gene and the former deposed chair as well as the eliminated program directors never appreciated what she tried to do. Their subsequent actions hurt and demeaned Gerri to the point that it affected her health.

In recent years terms for deans, provosts, and presidents reportedly declined in length. Twenty years in one office may have been counterproductive for this college as evidenced by what Gerri discovered: complacency, financial shortcomings, mission creep, and personnel concerns. Perhaps Gerri, the external hire, needed to view the college from a vantage point that the internal candidate could not see in order to address lingering issues as well as determine the general path down which to lead the whole unit. On the other hand, the internal candidate, Gene, knew the culture of the institution and the faculty over whom he would be presiding. Both arguments offer strong reasons to hire either candidate. One may read between the lines and wonder if upper administration and members of the search committee wanted Gerri to clean house knowing that an internal candidate may be less inclined to do so. Faculty who favored her rival, Gene, may contend that Gerri had been chosen because of her gender rather than her proven track record.

While courtesy is often extended to internal candidates like Gene, there should be no guarantee that the process results in his hiring but that the best candidate is selected. In this case strong internal support for Gene and the feeling that *he* would be hired set the tone for Gerri's stress-laden deanship probably before she moved into her office. She persevered nonetheless as she addressed problems and concerns. Gene's existing power base probably expected consolations for their support which stopped with Gerri's hiring. As a result, their efforts may have gone underground and continued to heighten her stress level.

Hot-headed Dean

Dave came to campus after having served as dean at two other institutions. His connections in the political world and in the professional realm made him highly marketable. Pressured by disappointments in his personal life and changes taking place in the college, however, Dave became a problem drinker. One new faculty member, Blair, challenged his new policy for travel allocations so Dave pushed him against a wall and told him to get with the program. Dave scolded another senior professor, Darlene, who challenged his understanding of total quality management by shaking his finger in her face and telling her to be a good little girl or else. In an exit interview, he told a departing tenured colleague, Valerie, who boldly told him why she was leaving that perhaps she could fix problems in her new job as there were no problems here. Dave became so mad at a visiting speaker, Hugh, that after challenging Hugh in the discussion following his speech, Dave followed him out to the parking lot to berate him further.

No one would condone or excuse Dave's actions toward his faculty. While his drinking may explain them, Dave has a problem that needs immediate attention before it escalates any further. In the meantime, his skills and abilities as a sitting dean cannot be utilized if he continues to treat his faculty in this uncivil and unacceptable manner. Not only does Dave attack his faculty but also outsiders who disagree with his policies or positions. If these faculty members share these instances with colleagues, potentially, Dave will lose credibility. He cannot lead people and programs or fulfill mission and vision under these circumstances.

If these incidents remain isolated no one has a grasp on the reality of the situation and fail to see it as something personal or health related. Undoubtedly, although not excusing his behavior, Dave, like other deans, experiences high levels of stress from personal and/or professional areas. However, Dave masked the problem with the hope perhaps that others would think it was organizational. In any case, he failed to acknowledge problems in his college by exclaiming to Valerie that there were none. Dave's world began to spin out of control as his focus shifted from moving the college forward to dealing with his personal demons.

More importantly, who stands in or wishes to take a position to suggest solutions to Dave's problems? Treating faculty like he did surely kept everyone at arm's length. The university may have formulated policy on substance abuse and what can be done about it but only after it is identified. In this case Dave's abuse also culminated in workplace harassment for which the university likely did not have a policy.

DEBRIEFING FACULTY/ADMINISTRATIVE RELATIONSHIPS

The department culture and the department chair/head share responsibility for socializing and integrating faculty into the department (Gallos, 2002; Waltman, Bergom, Hollenshead, Miller, & August, 2012). Bedeian (2002) noted that the dean upholds the college mission, communicates with faculty, effectively uses his or her power and authority, explains his or her rationale for decisions, and distributes resources fairly and equitably. But incumbents in both roles also expect reciprocal and collegial assistance and response from faculty. As the vignettes illustrated, faculty and administration must work in tandem rather than in opposition to each other to maximize outcomes.

Lessor (2008) reminded us that "organizational life is best understood by seeking out and presenting multiple perspectives" (p. 116). She suggested we use sociological principles to define the situation in which we find ourselves *and also* locate our position within that organization and its relationship to other positions. She recommended that the dean comprehend the history of the school in order to frame and reframe activities in the organization that move it forward. To illustrate, Lessor noted that different generations of faculty uphold slightly different goals and value systems. Furthermore, teaching, research, and service may be important to all faculty but the degree of importance each holds for faculty members differs. The job as dean necessitates a bridge between the generational views in order to reduce conflict.

Bray (2008) conducted a study of faculty normative expectations for dean behavior and categorized dean behaviors that faculty considered undesirable. Those behaviors faculty identified as reprehensible included "failure to follow established campus guidelines, poor communication, misappropriation of funds, and failure to confront rule violators" (p. 701). Additional behaviors that concerned faculty included a dean's failure to uphold the mission, the dean's ignoring shared governance opportunities, whitewashing issues instead of resolving them, and harshly and openly critiquing faculty. Faculty also discussed lesser infractions as unapproachability, not staying abreast of faculty research, and failing to fulfill one's vision. In a subsequent study Bray (2010) gained additional information on how faculty interprets dean behavior. Those behaviors that faculty regarded as high crimes include ineptitude with regard to various types of evaluation, failure of deans to communicate with faculty and not seek their input, disdain for deans who violate rules, failure of deans to punish rule breakers, and dean's lack of knowledge about formal regulations of promotion and tenure.

Department heads/chairs must understand their role as well as the parameters of their position. They may follow written procedures and policies in an administrative handbook or they may act capriciously, impulsively, and inconsistently (Hecht, 2004). Chairs/Heads indicate they are stressed as a result of "their unfamiliarity with the administrative system" and do not have sufficient information at entry, but rarely ask for or have time to attend professional development options (Carroll & Wolverton, 2004, p. 7). Ironically, a faculty career path is not necessarily preparation for the role of chair but appears always a prerequisite to it. Although leadership skill and training should be prerequisites to the chair/head position, newly installed faculty qua chairs/heads may possess neither.

With or without formal training and before administrators take action, they need to reflect on the rippling or chilling effect that their actions will have on others (Gunsalus, 2006). For instance, Dave, the dean, and Mickey, the chair, acted capriciously and without regard to their programs or their faculty. They failed to act in tandem.

When Gerri attempted to resolve a series of problems and she realized the reaction of her faculty made the job extremely difficult, she needed to try a different approach (Gunsalus, 2006). On the other hand, Meyerson (2003) and Kezar (2012) may depict Gerri as a tempered radical. While in the process of enacting change, Gerri experienced psychological stress that manifested itself in health issues. It became difficult for her to initiate what her peers believed to be radical changes within the college and equally difficult for Gerri to uphold her goals and values given their resistance. Perhaps she acted too soon without taking time to understand the culture into which she had entered. This culture undergirded the actions of her predecessor but sharply contrasted with her ideals and vision for the college (Bolman & Gallos, 2011; Gallos, 2002; Gunsalus, 2006).

FACULTY AND ADMINISTRATOR RELATIONSHIPS

Her rival had a clear advantage in this regard as he knew how to maneuver through the culture, but had he been hired initially, he may have perpetuated the status quo.

MacFarlane (2011) noted dissonance between faculty's perceptions of administrators' roles and how faculty relates to administration often making the role, actions, and reactions difficult to fathom. Although the collegium *is* the university, professors felt "excluded from the life of the university," particularly in "contributing toward its leadership and management" (MacFarlane, 2011, p. 71). This may come as a result of the business model being imposed on academe. This necessitated the need to socialize future faculty and prepare faculty for administrative roles differently than we did in the past. MacFarlane encouraged the need for mentoring and professional development commensurate with this paradigm shift. Gmelch (2004), however, advocated for general leadership development of faculty rather than specialized professional development that might be too focused on a particular administrative role.

Cramer (2006) summarized that new faculty rarely succeed if they "begin their careers with optimism or terror, with many good intentions or a belief that without too much effort, they could get by" (p. 528). In reality, there seems to be no guarantees for the group in the middle either. She attributed much of this to the relationships faculty have with their chair/head and dean. The chair/head especially serves as the key to faculty success because they are supposed to offer support and information, encourage faculty development, and suggest mentoring.

THE REST OF THE STORY

Ruth and Tyanne enjoyed the conference. Ruth represented the program on the board the following year just as the dean promised. Mickey struggled at the conference, stepped down as chair later that year, and never attended that conference again. Dick managed to alienate more tenured faculty who rallied to Christine's rescue, forcing Dick to reassess his role as department head. By the following year, Dick and Christine resolved their differences and worked in a more collegial fashion. Because of her health issues due mainly to stress, Gerri exited the dean's office with her head held high knowing she left the college in better shape than she found it. Poised and ready following her departure, Gene succeeded her. Dave finally checked into a rehab facility and he successfully addressed his drinking problem. Blair, Valerie, and Darlene found jobs elsewhere.

BEST PRACTICES

- Deans as well as chairs/heads must maintain close touch with their faculty and support efforts that allow his or her college to function corporately and effectively (Bray, 2008). Silverman (2004) suggested that good faculty–administrator relationships necessitate administrators to be service oriented in their demeanor, to grasp reality, hear all the facts, be positive, accept constructive criticism graciously, encourage their faculty to grow, to be flexible, and to delegate. Faculty need to know what roles these administrators should be playing during various faculty career stages.

- Taking a sociological perspective, faculty should construct cognitive maps of their departmental reality. These maps can be tools to help them visualize the lay of the land, specifically of personnel as well as issues, problems, and concerns. Try to mesh multiple maps together with other colleagues. Thomas and Schuh (2004) suggested that it is helpful to know the power brokers, the change agents, and the isolated faculty in their department. A sociogram would illustrate this beautifully and show various roles faculty play and with whom they interact frequently and infrequently (and why).

- Del Favero (2006) suggested that how faculty approach their research and scholarly work provides a model for how they may find greater knowledge of administrative expectations. For instance, use the old management-by-walking-around tactic: Be visible but also be unobtrusive. Observe what is going on. Communicate frequently with colleagues and administrators. Notice what behavior patterns are developing among faculty and between faculty and chairs/heads. Note how faculty interact with, or avoid, one another. Keep a journal of key observations. Thomas and Schuh (2004) strongly recommended that "keeping a finger on the pulse of the department is vital" (p. 24) and faculty already have the researching tools to accomplish this.

RESOURCES

- The AAUP website contains the following link to information on contingent faculty and supplies the reader with resources to assist this group of professionals: www.aaup.org/AAUP/issues/contingent/. *Academic Leader* is an online newsletter that faculty and prospective department chairs may find helpful: www.magnapubs.com/newsletter/academic-leader/. *The Department Chair* offers additional information to assist faculty contemplating the chair position: http://onlinelibrary.wiley.com/journal/10.1002/(ISSN)1936-4393. If faculty wish to know the basic expectations for their department head/chair with respect to new and mid-career faculty, they should read current publications on that role (Hecht, 2004): Denton and Brown's (2009) *A Practical Guide to University and College Management* offers faculty information on practical ways that administrators navigate through their role. The American Association of Higher Education sponsored Sorcinelli's (2000) *Principles of Good Practice* and AAUP's and the American Council on Education's co-produced *Good Practice in Tenure Evaluation* (2000) also assist faculty with deciphering administrative roles and expectations.

99

Chapter 10
Off the Tenure Track
With Janice Epstein, *Texas A&M University*

INTRODUCTION

Unfortunately, as higher education becomes more corporatized and subject to budget cuts, non-tenure track faculty percentages will continue to rise. Gravios (2006) reported that in 2003, 46 percent of faculty worked part-time. In 2007, 49 percent of faculty worked part-time and 12 percent worked full-time but off the tenure track (Clawson, 2009). Kezar (2012) reported that 66 percent of faculty work off the tenure track; the AAUP estimates this group to be as numerous as 68 percent (www.aaup.org/AAUP/issues/contingent/contingentfacts.htm); and the Association of American Colleges and University (AACU) feels non-tenure track appointments have reached 70 percent (www.aacu.org/peerreview/pr-su12/RealityCheck.cfm).

Hurt (2011) found the treatment of non-tenure track faculty women to vary across departments but their status often rendered them peripheral, marginal, and vulnerable. Any faculty working off the tenure track may be titled or labeled by their institution or department any of the following terms: lecturers, instructors, adjuncts, or clinical faculty; at-will, fixed-term, contingent, non-tenure eligible, or contract faculty; scholar-in-residence or visiting scholar; invisible, non-status, or silent faculty; and freeway fliers or gypsy scholars (Hurt, 2011; Kezar & Sam, 2010). Some titles explain the role while others offer a more derogatory label.

Only one vignette appears in this chapter but it contains several layers and themes discussed through multiple lenses. Each illustrated the issues faced by a female faculty member who works off the tenure track, teaching full-time while assuming quasi-administrative roles. Without tenure, she fell victim to capricious administrative decisions, colleague incivility, health issues, and disengagement (Huston, Norman, & Ambrose, 2007; Namie & Namie, 2000; Twale & De Luca, 2008).

Unresolved Conflict

Duncan, the department head, had his hands full with tenured faculty member, Humphrey, and non-tenure track, long-term senior lecturer, Karen. Over the years, Humphrey had a history of berating Karen and accusing her of stepping outside her bounds of authority. Karen defended herself, but to no avail. When Karen's immediate supervisor left the university, Humphrey assumed the role of associate department head. Karen contacted Duncan following several new incidents and Duncan agreed to speak to Humphrey. In an email, Duncan informed Karen that, "No matter what the outcomes, I want you to know that I have the highest regard for your teaching and your many contributions to the department."

Duncan emailed Karen again saying, "Humphrey and I met to discuss your introductory course coordinator (ICC) position. I indicated to him that your recent activities were consistent with what the pervious associate head expected, but according to Humphrey, they do not appear to be in line with his current vision of the position. Humphrey is now pondering what the role of the ICC should be (if any), and then he and I will talk again." Subsequently, Karen became so intimidated by further encounters with Humphrey that she avoided interaction with him and reluctantly resigned from her administrative duties as ICC.

The existence of a tense, strained, non-collegial relationship between colleagues that have worked in the department for an extended period of time is evident here. Although tensions emerged before Humphrey became associate head of the department, they escalated as he utilized his new position as a legitimate platform from which to continue negative behaviors toward Karen. Because department head, Duncan, failed to address the problems initially, animosities continued rather than subsided. He should have realized that Humphrey's appointment rendered Karen more vulnerable now. Duncan needed to intervene and discuss with Humphrey the bounds of his authority over Karen. Duncan chose instead to placate Karen even though he knew Humphrey's unrelenting animosity toward her persisted.

Humphrey and Karen worked on a state educational grant as co-principle investigators. Although she presumed she was fulfilling her duties, Humphrey yelled at Karen informing her she acted in direct contradiction to what he asked her to do. In a subsequent encounter that Karen taped, Humphrey contradicted his previous directive. Humphrey told Karen, "You can accept me and the fact that I am the associate head . . . or not. You do things and then you make up excuses afterward. You have a PhD and don't you know what is important and what is not?" Subsequently, Karen spoke to Duncan again and together they devised a plan to prevent future incidents with Humphrey from happening.

Gender/Sexual harassment for which university policy exists is not the issue here. Humphrey's actions loomed under the radar of sexual harassment because his behavior toward Karen was work related rather than specifically associated with gender. Whatever efforts Duncan alone or in conjunction with Karen devised were not carried out so

Duncan needed to continue to work with Humphrey and Karen individually and together until their problems were resolved. Inability to bring these two parties to some consensus only allowed the problems to fester. Perhaps the absence of policy and/or sanction reinforced Humphrey's subsequent incidents of uncivil behavior toward Karen and left Duncan without a viable way to help her.

When Karen asked Humphrey via email about her duties for the spring semester, Humphrey requested to speak to her in person but Karen asked a colleague to accompany her. During that meeting, Humphrey verbally attacked Karen, which was acknowledged by her colleague. Subsequently, Karen met with the associate dean of faculties with the intent to initiate a college grievance action against Humphrey. Administration assured Karen that there would be no retaliation allowed following her request. However, just after Humphrey received Karen's request for mediation from the committee, he established a three-person committee of his own to review the use of Karen's co-authored introductory textbook. Humphrey loaded the committee with his allies.

Because of Duncan's seeming inaction on Karen's behalf, her own response to Humphrey began with a paper trail of emails and continued with a taping of their conversation. Oddly, some damning comments made by Humphrey in those emails indicated precisely his demeaning posture toward her. While these emails would benefit Karen because they documented Humphrey's behavior, they registered little clout with Duncan, the dean, or the grievance committee. With future communications, Karen insisted wisely that everything be in writing, that there be limited interaction between her and Humphrey, and when necessary, there should be a third party present in those interactions.

Wisely, Karen involved her department head first *and then* the associate dean of faculties when it became apparent that Duncan's efforts on her behalf failed to address the issues. There is no indication when, how, and if Duncan informed the dean or associate dean of the problems between Karen and Humphrey formally or informally. As a result, she tried to resolve the issue herself rather than hold Duncan accountable. Karen sought impartial assistance through her valued colleague who validated her claims against Humphrey. Unfortunately, the promise of pursuing mediation came with a no-retaliation assurance. This may have allegedly been violated causing Karen to remain in a vulnerable position, unprotected by the associate dean of faculties, Duncan, or the dean. Regardless of the validity of Karen's assertion of retaliation, it was very real to her (Gunsalus, 2006).

While such peer evaluations are common, regular, and expected in academe, the questionable timing of a possibly contrived evaluation of Karen's textbook by Humphrey's committee served to obscure peer review and disguise the exercise as perhaps retaliation for Karen's pushing for mediation (Kekes, 1996). Humphrey probably felt that Karen brought this on herself by her reactions to his actions

(Gunsalus, 2006). To neutralize the situation, Duncan should have postponed the peer review of Karen's introductory textbook until the conflicts between Karen and Humphrey had been resolved or until the grievance committee had rendered a decision on the mediation. Selecting more impartial committee members to review the textbook or canceling it altogether were options for Duncan.

The College Grievance Committee advocated for mediation rather than initiate grievance proceedings. They believed that in order to maintain the integrity of the services provided by the department the issue needed to be resolved and needed to be done so quickly. Because Humphrey exercised his prerogative to not voluntarily participate in mediation, the committee concurred that Duncan, the department head, and perhaps the dean should have taken care of the problem before it escalated to this point. In their message to the dean, the committee recommended that Duncan or the dean secure Humphrey's participation. Barring that, the dean and Duncan should become actively involved in the mediation process themselves.

The university website describes mediation as a process of resolving inevitable conflicts that arise between colleagues. That should have been a signal to Duncan and the dean that perhaps an intervention with Karen and Humphrey should have been attempted much earlier. Duncan may have felt that another administrative body intervened on Karen's behalf and that takes the pressure off him *and* his dean. There is no indication that Duncan sought any assistance through Human Resources or spoke with Humphrey prior to or following Karen's request for mediation. On the other hand, if the university did not have any policies in place that addressed workplace harassment, there is probably little Duncan could do formally. Just because the formal policy is not there, however, does not absolve Duncan of some responsibility for defusing the situation.

The dean claimed that Duncan, the department head, continued to work on the situation, however, nothing seemed to result from the department head's office. When Karen's teaching schedule that Humphrey finalized proved to be her worst ever since joining the department, she filed a university grievance. Eventually, the College Grievance Committee met with the previous associate department head and also Duncan and Humphrey. Karen knew of other non-tenure track department colleagues who also experienced frequent harassment, but they did not feel comfortable filing a similar grievance against Humphrey, so Karen moved forward on her own. The case did not end in Karen's favor. Shortly thereafter, Humphrey stepped into Karen's office doorway and cautioned, "If you ever go after me again, I will take you to court." Karen felt the emotional strain and job stress take its toll when the ordeal manifested itself in an anxiety attack that she mistook for a heart attack.

Duncan had inadvertently supported Humphrey's conduct because nothing transpired to alter it or stop it. Personal insults via email needed to be dealt with swiftly rather than escalating to mediation. Duncan knew about it, showed support for Karen, and appeased her by suggesting tactful ways to assist her. By all indications, Duncan failed to successfully address the issue immediately and directly. Even though he talked to Humphrey after the first request from Karen, a second request occurred for which we are unsure if there was a repeat discussion. In a second discussion, Duncan needed to express greater intolerance for Humphrey's behavior. Not listening to both sides of the problem from Humphrey *and* Karen as a group exercise indicates that Duncan did not collect as much data as he needed to collect, if he truly intended to address the issue. We do not know the dialogue from the first meeting between Duncan and Humphrey but we do know that Humphrey's behavior remained unmodified as a result of that meeting as evidenced by his subsequent emails to Karen. The situation eventually digressed into a he said/she said encounter such that "both sides projected motives onto the other that fostered the caricature necessary to support their own claims" (Harris & Hartley, 2011, p. 713).

Duncan probably did not condone Humphrey's behavior, but he did little to stop it or to resolve the issues that persisted. Duncan may have been preoccupied with running a very large department, keeping it functional at the expense of defusing conflict situations like the ongoing relationship between Humphrey and Karen. His perceptions of the situation indicated that he did not see poor collegial relationships as potentially affecting his goals, or if he did, desired to do nothing about them, or simply did not know what to do. There is no indication of the dean's concern as to how Duncan handled (or mishandled) the situation even though Duncan occupied the best position to monitor faculty behavior. Perhaps Duncan could have listened to Karen's colleague who witnessed Humphrey's behavior firsthand; but that did not happen either. Without a systemic effort to resolve this conflict, Duncan would have difficulty convincing non-tenure track faculty that he advocated for them in the department.

DEBRIEFING OFF THE TENURE TRACK

Duncan had several courses of action. Removing Humphrey or not renewing Karen's contract appeared to be simple, short-term solutions to immediate problems. Even though chairs possess the power to renew or discontinue non-tenure track contracts (Hutchens, 2011), as senior lecturer, Karen had proven herself and should not, therefore, be dismissed. Furthermore, no *official* evidence existed to indicate that Humphrey's behavior toward Karen extended to others in the department or that he failed to perform *his* assigned duties.

In the early stages, neither Duncan nor the dean took responsibility for resolving the problem. This may be due to lack of policy, *their* individual relationships with Karen and Humphrey, and/or their superficial knowledge and experience with such issues. Nothing and no one held either administrator accountable for finding a solution in a timely fashion (Hecht, 2004). We are not sure to what extent these administrators worked or allied together or made this issue an administrative priority. If Duncan and the dean collaborated on how to resolve this issue, their suggestions failed to help Karen directly or to modify Humphrey's behavior. They had the potential to work together to defuse the situation before it went to mediation or grievance but neither took responsibility. In fact, the College Grievance Committee lightly admonished them for not acting judiciously *before* the situation affected the services provided to the students in the department.

Karen's colleagues within the department could address this issue but did not, especially other non-tenure track appointees. As marginal and perhaps vulnerable citizens of the department, they chose perhaps reluctantly not to involve themselves in the circumstances (Baldwin & Chronister, 2001; Kezar & Sam, 2011). Perhaps this gave Duncan a false sense that he oversaw a more functional department, therefore, he felt justified offering minimal action to resolve this conflict. However, ignoring any warning signals early in a problem's development almost ensures escalation (Gunsalus, 2006). Even when Duncan knew about the situation, he allowed Karen and Humphrey's conflict to persist. Faculty members should have voiced their displeasure with the uncivil action of their peers; tenured faculty members may have to act on behalf of their non-tenure track or untenured colleagues but in this case they did not (Gunsalus, 2006; Twale & De Luca, 2008).

While the College Grievance Committee indicated that there *may* be a problem, they probably did not want to make it *their* problem. Furthermore, the College Grievance Committee proved even less accommodating to Karen. Hearing only the administration's views seemed to suppress some pertinent information from Karen's peers even if that suppression followed policy. According to Gunsalus (2006), it becomes "the central right to confront the evidence and to have a chance to rebut it . . . [but] not every proceeding requires confrontation of witnesses" (p. 152). However, they concluded that the long-term animosity between Karen and Humphrey had the potential to disrupt the mission and integrity of the department. But their ruling did not resolve Karen's situation.

Gunsalus (2006) noted several typical responses to uncivil behavior including "avoidance . . . denial, appeasement, negotiation, [and] mediation" (p. 122). This department witnessed all of these in varying degrees. Furthermore, Gunsalus confirmed that "academics seem to find it particularly difficult to raise troublesome topics, especially ones involving the personal conduct of a colleague" (p. 127) and, in this case, someone working in an administrative capacity. This vignette incorporated the drama generated through the filing of a faculty grievance but concluded with the hope associated with re-engagement to the collegium by a non-tenure track faculty member. The ruling did not necessarily accomplish this goal.

In their study of non-tenure track faculty, Waltman et al. (2012) recognized that some participants desired to fly under the radar so as not to stir any type of controversies that would jeopardize their jobs. Participants also revealed that their fate—hire or fire—rested specifically with their department chair/head so they remained cautious about their relationship with him or her. Levin and Shaker (2011) described non-tenure track faculty members as taking on the persona of a chameleon in that they work in an academic culture and are not really a part of it, but rather are peripheral to or detached from it. Their desire to be team players and good citizens may be thwarted by their precarious status and their colleagues' perceptions of that status. As a result, non-tenure track faculty may have to re-envision their role to suit the prevailing culture.

Karen differed from the typical non-tenure track faculty member discussed in the literature. She challenged her new associate department head knowing their already strained relationship (Bedeian, 2002). Karen began to advocate for herself, that is, become her own advocate and agent in the absence of assistance from reluctant untenured colleagues and the administration (Twale & De Luca, 2008). She would not allow the boundaries of her non-tenure track status to stop her agency (Levin & Shaker, 2011). As is typically the case, Karen suffered personally the brunt of the problem in the process with little or no negative consequences befalling Humphrey, Duncan, the dean, or the associate dean of faculties (Harris & Hartley, 2011).

THE REST OF THE STORY

Given her seniority and good yearly performance appraisals, Karen's awful teaching schedule indicated that Humphrey may be attempting to retaliate further. To self-advocate, Karen ran for faculty senate. Successful, she joined the Senate Personnel and Welfare Committee and began working with senate colleagues on a university workplace harassment policy. The faculty senate unanimously passed the policy, which was signed two months later by the university president. It awaits implementation as a Standard Administrative Procedure. Karen's campus now employs a full-time faculty ombudsperson. All new department chairs must participate in conflict resolution training. Karen's case proved to be the impetus for these changes. Humphrey resigned from the university to pursue other interests.

BEST PRACTICES

- Faculty and department chairs need a detailed characterization of the collegial culture of their department. Their mental model of the department frames how they respond to situations (Stanley & Algert, 2007). The faculty along with the chair should monitor the department culture, level of collegiality, and climate in order to address problems that arise. Getting at the root of any problem or conflict is imperative for defusing a situation (Gunsalus, 2006). An outside consultant may also be able to determine impartially the socio-cultural nature of a department.

- Due to the rise in the filing of faculty/administrative grievances, an increasing number of campuses have appointed a faculty ombudsperson to intervene. Resolving escalating disputes and conflicts before they get out of control means ombudspersons intervene early *and* advocate for faculty. Karen could have contacted that official immediately for advice and assistance if her university had one initially. Ombudspersons play significant roles especially when the uncivil behavior occurs between superiors and direct subordinates as well as between colleagues (Gunsalus, 2006).

- Institutions that conduct workshops and professional development should consider a unit on working collegially as well as on conflict management and resolution (Stanley & Algert, 2007).

- Non-tenure track faculty sits in a vulnerable position. Suggestions for addressing this vulnerability can be found in Twale and De Luca (2008). The focus in this case seemed to be Karen's initiatives to remedy her *own* situation. This is the only thing over which she had control. However, the focus should have been with remedying the conflict situation in so far as Karen may not have been the only victim or her predicament the only conflict. Her situation may have been symptomatic of other unrelated issues and dysfunctions within the department (Gunsalus, 2006). It took Karen's trip to the grievance committees to pick up on this.

- If campuses do not have sections in their faculty handbook or a separate handbook for non-tenure track hires, they should consider this, especially as the number of full- and part-time faculty employed off the tenure track continue to rise (Kezar & Sam, 2010, 2011).

- In addition, offering campus-wide consistency in non-tenure track faculty titles, orientation offerings, professional development, contract wording, expectations, compensation, and benefits would be beneficial to this faculty group (Kezar & Sam, 2011).

RESOURCES

- The AAUP website contains the following link to information on contingent faculty and supplies the reader with resources to assist this group of faculty professionals at www.aaup.org/AAUP/issues/contingent/. *Academic Leader* is an online newsletter that provides information on conflict resolution at www.magnapubs.com/newsletter/academic-leader/. The National Center for Educational Statistics reports information on post-secondary employees including tenure and off tenure track appointments that will assist universities with monitoring tenure and non-tenure track faculty ratios at http://nces.ed.gov/pubsearch.pdf.

Chapter 11

Pathways to Full Professor

INTRODUCTION

Once tenure and promotion from assistant to associate professor occurs, mid-career faculty must serve time-in-rank (which may vary from institution to institution) before placing their credentials up for promotion to full professor. While promotion to associate often means an involuntary and mandatory career step, the decision to seek full professor is purely voluntary. Thus, many faculty never espouse nor seek the rank of full. Because scholarship plays a more significant factor in the promotion process to full, especially at research institutions, the pipeline tends to narrow as tenured faculty choose between several career options. These include consulting, increasing service involvement on campus and professional service off campus, applying for administrative positions, and/or placing a greater emphasis on teaching and student advising. For faculty pursuing the rank of full, national and international recognition garnered from publishing, presenting, and journal editing must be demonstrated. Faculty must also seek support for their advancement to full rank from their colleagues on campus as well as have their dossier examined and assessed by external reviewers off campus. These full professors must be well known in the field in which the candidate publishes and hold tenure at a comparable university classification. Sounds simple but the vignettes below illustrate otherwise.

Rich's Promotion to Full—First and Second Chances

For years the dean insisted that anyone going up for promotion to full professor must have a published book, however, this expectation failed to make it into the P&T document. Having been an associate professor for more than a decade, Rich submitted his dossier to the committee. He had many publications but no book. Even though he had chair and faculty support, Rich did not secure promotion as the dean held tightly to his expectations. Deciding to not appeal the decision, Rich decided instead to write a book proposal, which he pitched to several academic publishers at national conferences he attended. Finally, Rich secured a signed contract from a reputable publisher. Three years passed before Rich's book hit the shelves. Because so many colleagues supported him through the lengthy process, Rich personally thanked them and proudly sent each of them an inscribed complimentary copy of his new book. When it came time to resubmit his credentials for promotion to full, Rich felt confident he presented a stronger case to his voting colleagues, the same ones who had supported him through the book writing phase. He anticipated the newly hired dean and his chair would also support him. He had no reason to believe otherwise. Outside support from three nationally respected colleagues in his field overwhelmingly supported Rich's candidacy.

As word came down from the provost's office on the hill, Rich sank in his office chair. He learned that the majority of the faculty did not vote in support of his promotion to full. Letters from the chair and dean tended to be lukewarm and thus did not strongly support Rich either. Offering his sincere apologies to Rich, the provost encouraged him to try again in a year or two. Shaken not stirred, Rich wondered why his colleagues, chair, and dean voted as they had.

It would not be unusual for the dean or the faculty culture of a school to expect that candidates seeking full professor would have needed to write a book but the expectation also needed to be stated in the P&T document. For Rich to submit his credentials the first time without the book seemed perfectly reasonable assuming he met the stated criteria in the published document. In his second attempt, Rich fulfilled the dean's unwritten expectation with a singly authored text highlighting his expertise published by a reputable academic publisher. His external letters of support noted his accomplishments. But in the meantime, that dean retired and a new one took office. Rich encountered difficulty within his department that could possibly be political in nature given the fact that the chair supported him earlier. Rich also received little support from faculty who verbally told him earlier they did. He amassed strong support from outside reviewers in his field, which obviously contradicted the views of his department. In this case, it would be difficult to determine why department colleagues and the chair failed to support him at this point in time. The newly installed dean probably went along with the prevailing sentiment that favored the faculty and chair. Rich felt that he had done everything he was asked to do and more as the P&T document never changed to reflect the need for a book. Rich wondered whether waiting for a couple more years and trying again, although an option many candidates encounter, would make any difference so long as the colleagues, chair, and dean remained the same.

Margie's Promotion to Full—First and Second Chances

At Margie's university, one needed to be an associate professor for at least four years before going up for full professor. During those years, she asked several full professors in her department how many publications they considered adequate for promotion to full. Margie consistently heard 30 refereed publications would be expected. Following the four-year wait time, she compiled an impressive dossier with over 30 refereed publications, good classroom evaluations, and consistent service to the university, department, and her profession.

When the four full professors met to review and deliberate the merits of her credentials, they unanimously voted 'no.' The chair relayed the message to Margie but stated he would support her as would the dean if she decided to go further. However, the chair noted that one of her three letters of external support seemed lukewarm which may cause a problem with the university committee. Margie decided to postpone the process until the next year when one of the four full professors in her department would be retired. She may stand a better chance with just three voting colleagues. The following year she resubmitted her file with three new professional letters of support and more publications. In the meantime, she secured a book contract.

During this second attempt the remaining three full professors voted this time to abstain. Two other colleagues submitted their credentials that year, too. The male candidate, Steve, whose credentials were similar to Margie's, received a unanimous vote of no. The female candidate, Linda, whose credentials showed no publications since she received tenure 15 years earlier, but who planned to retire at the end of the academic year, was supported unanimously for promotion.

Disappointed and confused, Margie swallowed the vote but this time sent her credentials forward to the university committee. With overwhelming support from three new outside reviewers, the chair, and the dean, she felt more confident this time.

Margie, like Rich, asked colleagues about the expectation within their department culture for promotion to full. Faculty seeking promotion to full probably have enough savvy to know whom to ask. Similarly, these candidates reside within the culture long enough to know who is likely to vote 'yes' and who may vote 'no.' In each instance, the candidate reached the stated or implied expectations. In each instance, however, they met opposition and were denied full status one or more times. Were Margie's first and second outcomes the result of politics, too? To know and read the culture are important. In Margie's department, senior colleagues expected that candidates would approach them informally asking for their support. Margie asked her colleagues what she needed to have accomplished in her dossier but she did not go so far as *to ask for* their support. Within this culture, to ask for their support created an obligatory relationship. She would be forever beholden to them. Margie took her chances when she decided not to play their political game.

To be fair, the lukewarm external letter could have been enough for the first vote to be 'no.' However, the stellar letters coupled with a better dossier the second time resulted in an abstention, which makes little sense. And the fact that both votes were unanimous seems odd enough to presume that Margie *was* being blocked from securing promotion for political reasons. Margie did not ask for permission and colleague support because it would have created an obligatory relationship that would have played out in the second vote. The voting professors knew she exceeded the expectations for full but sent her a message with the abstentions. Unlike Rich's predicament, Margie had the support of her chair and dean both times. The faculty vote did not sway administrative support of Margie. Rich presumed he also had administrative support, and in fact may have had it, that is, until the majority of faculty voted not to support him. The full professors probably presumed that, regardless of their vote, Margie would send her credentials to the university committee so the unanimous abstention rather than another 'no' vote allowed them to save face while still expressing their views. Given that Margie would not be beholden to them if she made full without their support probably made them a bit uneasy. As a full professor Margie would have the ability, albeit legitimate power, to say what she felt in opposition to the other full professors, to garner department support in opposition to them, and to redirect the department climate over time. They probably dreaded the thought but could not ultimately stop it.

Steve's Promotion to Full—Last Chance

After several unsuccessful attempts for promotion to full, Steve decided he would give it one last shot before he planned to retire in a few years. Steve amassed a significant number of refereed publications, and his service commitments and teaching evaluations were where they needed to be. Steve, unlike Margie, decided to talk to each of the three professors voting on his credentials. He wanted to find out if they felt he was indeed a viable candidate and if they supported his candidacy. Two colleagues assured him he was ready and they pledged their support. The third colleague expressed doubt that Steve would be successful now any more than he had been the last several times he went up for full.

As mentioned in the previous vignette, Steve failed to secure any positive votes and thus his application was denied yet again because the chair and dean proved to be less supportive than he needed in this circumstance. He expressed grave disappointment that he was once again overlooked in favor of Linda who had not published much at all, especially recently. He had a consistent record of publication over his tenure at the institution. Steve expressed sincere congratulations to Margie. She concurred that Linda's promotion appeared to be a gift while Steve and Margie had worked consistently over the last several years to earn their promotion but had yet to be recognized. Margie and Steve talked over coffee and brainstormed why they thought these outcomes occurred. They discussed what recourse Steve may have.

Steve and Margie bonded over this matter collegially as they attempted to piece together what happened. Based on the departmental culture, they concluded that the results reflected a dysfunctional political climate that prevailed within the department. They believed that Linda received promotion because not only did she plan to retire and would be eligible for emeritus status but she socially interacted with all three members of the voting committee. She had been on the faculty longer than those members and perhaps they felt beholden to Linda. Clearly, her record did not meet the requirements stated in the document. The disparity between the three records and the three votes indicated to Steve and Margie that the committee evaluated each *person* rather than assessed the merits of their dossiers against the expected standards. Had the committee functioned fairly rather than politically, the votes would have been different.

DEBRIEFING PATHWAY TO FULL PROFESSOR

According to Ornstein, Stewart, and Drakich (2007), "promotion is a bureaucratically organized activity [that is] based on the collective judgments of colleagues, committees, and university officials" (p. 5). The perceptions of each of these groups can differ over time. What makes it more difficult is the absence of standards within the collegium. What prospective candidates do know is that they must establish a national and international reputation in their field/discipline that can more easily be interpreted through empirical research and an established scholarly record of presentation and especially publication (Mabrouk, 2007). But as Rich, Margie, and Steve learned, the prevailing climate in the department may block an otherwise stellar record for precarious political reasons not linked to the quality of the dossier. Linda's presence in the department's full professor club may not have threatened the members as much as Margie, Steve, or Rich may have in their respective departments.

An associate professor's informal expectations of his or her own career development factor heavily into the motivation needed for him or her to seek promotion to full (Britton, 2010; McDowell, Singell, & Ziliak, 2011). Because promotion to full is voluntary as opposed to promotion to associate, professors chart their own course. Linda presents a good example of someone who had no desire to seek promotion because she did not choose to publish after receiving tenure. In addition, Roach and El-Khawas (2010) alluded to a 'culture of privacy' among tenured mid-career faculty whose research and credentials tend to be infrequently, if at all, scrutinized by anyone but the department chair. In many cases with no clear-cut guidelines and/or a vague set of goals for associate professors, the interpretation of the process to promotion and the credentials rests with the department chair (Roach & El-Khawas, 2010). By all indications, the department chair should not have encouraged Linda to seek full professor given her record. Neither Margie nor Steve learned if the dean and department chair supported

Linda. They also wondered how Linda obtained the glowing external letters of support she needed.

Post-tenure faculty need as much direction and encouragement as those in the pre-tenure stage. Once institutions award tenure, they typically assume faculty will, as mature professionals, continue to take on more service and quasi-administrative roles (Baldwin, DeZure, Shaw, & Moretto, 2008). These faculty either land onto a confusing plateau that forces them to reassess their goals and research agendas or rest on a comfortable side street coasting along until retirement. Changes within their respective disciplines/fields, puzzling technologies, and different generations of students pose challenges to mid-career faculty that necessitate a higher level of motivation and competitive edge in order for them to remain on the cutting edge. To avoid the onset of deadwood status, department chairs/heads and deans must address the predicament that mid-career faculty often face (Baldwin et al., 2008). For Rich's dean to suggest that awarding full professor must first result in a book publication fully supports Baldwin's premise but the faculty must agree to write it into the P&T document before it becomes gospel.

While the basic process for achieving full professor exists in the faculty handbook, each department needs to specify its unwritten expectations of faculty who seek to achieve this rank (Baldwin et al., 2008). Most university policies are mysterious and intentionally vague for full professor because disciplinary expectations tend to be set within the department or college (Weiser, 2012). Nowhere in Margie's, Steve's, or Linda's faculty handbook did a 30-publication minimum appear. Margie's colleagues arbitrarily established it at that. In the Field, Barg, and Stallings (2011) study mid-career respondents indicated a desire to receive constructive feedback from senior colleagues, an assessment of their progress, and critical guidance after reaching associate professor and before contemplating promotion to full. Margie, Steve, and Rich sought this information but found it inconsistent and, as it turned out, deceptive.

Typically though, criteria for full professor include national and international reputation (Weiser, 2012): an excellent and consistent record of research and publication including articles in peer-reviewed journals, book chapters, and books advancing one's discipline; effective teaching; and a varied record of campus and professional service and outreach activities (Baldwin et al., 2008). Internal review committees may not be able to evaluate their colleagues' accomplishments and must rely heavily on the expertise of external reviewers who bring balance and credibility to the evaluation. However, internal and external peer reviewers may use their *own* criteria to assess dossiers in lieu of relying on vaguely conceived university guidelines (Weiser, 2012).

At research institutions, excellence in research and either teaching or service must be demonstrated to a committee of one's peers (Roach & El-Khawas, 2010). In all cases, a full professorship reflects faculty leadership ability and professional stature on and off campus (Mabrouk, 2007). However, the expectations vary from department to department and across institutions at the rank of full making the process somewhat precarious.

One area extensively researched is the gender and racial disparity found among mid-career faculty seeking promotion to full professor (McDowell et al., 2011; Ornstein et al., 2007). Geisler, Kaminski, and Berkeley (2007) determined that promotion in rank varied by discipline or professional field. Their index looked at mid-career faculty and promotion to full and indicated problems within departments in terms of advancement, especially of women and minorities. That did not appear to be the case in these vignettes but could in others.

Buch et al. (2011) found that women more than men plateau at the associate level. Linda provides a good illustration. Several reasons emerged from their study including reactive versus proactive faculty development; lack of clear, consistent promotion criteria; and focus on limited paths to full professor. When women *do* opt for promotion like Margie, studies show it takes them one or two years longer than men to achieve it (Roach & El-Khawas, 2010). McDowell et al. (2011) noted that in the field of economics, for instance, women expressed a preference for teaching and service rather than research, which may explain their contented presence on that plateau.

THE REST OF THE STORY

Rich decided it was time to search for a faculty position elsewhere. Linda received promotion to full and retired from the university the following year. Margie obtained promotion on the second try despite the three abstentions. However, she was neither congratulated by her three colleagues nor surprised by their actions. Steve never made full before he retired from the university several years later.

BEST PRACTICES

- Newly tenured faculty should be required to create a mid-career plan that they share with their department chair/head and dean. Together they can function as a team to encourage peer mentoring, as well as provide direction, encouragement, development opportunities, and resources (Buch et al., 2011).

- Promotion documents should offer greater transparency and more explicit guidelines to mid-career faculty seeking promotion to full. Faculty preparing the document may also contemplate multiple pathways to this rank (Buch et al., 2011; Roach & El-Khawas, 2010). Field et al.'s (2011) findings suggested faculty desire to receive constructive and consistent feedback and critical guidance from senior colleagues in order for them to assess their progress to full. This should be done in conjunction with yearly performance appraisals to provide the candidate with consistency and guidance from the chair.

- Mid-career faculty anticipating the rank of full as well as contemplating leadership and/or management opportunities would benefit from campus and conference workshops and seminars as well as sabbaticals in order to pursue training and other opportunities to lead on and off campus (Baldwin et al., 2008).

- Surveying mid-career faculty on campus to learn of their needs should be school-wide or university-wide to determine any overlapping needs and interests (Baldwin et al., 2008; Field et al., 2011). Knowing what this faculty group needs will help match available campus resources and provide those needs through professional development.

RESOURCES

- The AAUP website offers information on maintaining faculty productivity after they receive tenure: www.aaup.org/AAUP/issues/tenure/productivity.htm. For additional information on the full professorship readers can access the Inside Higher Education website at http://insidehighered.com. Burnham, Hooper, and Wright's (2010) *Tools for Dossier Success* should also be helpful to faculty seeking full professor.

Epilog

Throughout this book, readers have followed the careers of various faculty members as they surmounted professional obstacles, triumphing over many or reassessing strategies to try again. Each chapter offered readers insight and possible avenues into how to deal with similar encounters as well as addressed the need to understand their academic cultures and act collegially. I close the book with final thoughts illustrated through the case vignette of two new characters, Jean and Myra.

After Jean graduated with her PhD, she traveled 800 miles to take a faculty position. She must have been from Venus as she truly landed on Mars. She struggled at first with little guidance from seasoned colleagues or the department chair. Shortly she joined forces with Myra, another junior faculty member experiencing the same things. Much of what they witnessed in faculty gatherings and university documents surprised, confused, and troubled them. They shared their observations with each other daily and tried to make sense of their cultural and organizational environment in order to preserve their own sanity and reach their professional goals.

For some departments, the tendency appears to hire new faculty and assume they will prosper. Because assistance, mentoring, and informal socialization vary by department, school, and university, faculty and administrations need to be better at monitoring new hires and their relationship with incumbent faculty (Lang, 2005). Unfortunately, new faculty like Jean and Myra tend not to ask for help with their teaching, research, or service expectations. In addition, they found policy to be vaguely written and interpreted loosely. Consistency in the explanation of expectations to new faculty is important to the success of entry level as well as mid-career faculty. The vignette should encourage senior colleagues and administrators to assist new hires like Jean and Myra rather than assume they have 'hit the ground running' and are unlikely to stumble.

Offering a graduate seminar or course such as the professoriate for future college professors could expose new faculty to the range of expectations and behaviors they may encounter (Bjorklund & Rehling, 2010). Neither Jean nor Myra had such a course. With or without this information, faculty new to a university must self-advocate, that is, know the organization and the faculty culture in the department. Jean and Myra became students of it. They used their research skills to research academe and, after sharing their findings with each other, discussed them in order to make sense of the data they gathered (Curry, 2000; Twale & De Luca, 2008). It worked but this is no substitute for collegial interaction and mentoring with their departmental colleagues.

Every department or college tries to camouflage problems or dysfunction (Beamish, 2000; Dzeich & Weiner, 1990; Gibson, 2006). Myra and Jean noted some departmental dysfunctions through their observations and discussions. When faculty or administration ignore the existence of problems or issues, it affects everyone, especially new hires. As a result, good faculty may leave the institution before the problems often do, if faculty and administration fail to address them. Preventing organizational pathology means identifying obvious dysfunctions before they dominate situations within a department culture and escalate further (Harris & Hartley, 2011). Ignoring seemingly 'harmless' situations may set greater problems in motion. Myra and Jean witnessed such events and often brainstormed in their discussions how they could have been handled more effectively. Llorens (2010) suggested sharing and disseminating all types of academic information with faculty and administrators. She called for educating members of the academic culture on how to speak up and address major issues, albeit in a collegial manner. On their paths to tenure Myra and Jean remained cautious in what they said publically, however, much to their chagrin. Permitting an academic culture of silence subverts the collegium and its purposes (Slevin, 1993). On occasion Myra and Jean were able to share their observations with administrators they trusted. To ensure participation, Llorens encouraged dialog and open communication over silence. Myra and Jean realized that this was much easier said than done.

Jean and Myra noted that dysfunctional issues became more difficult to resolve once instituted in their department. Modifying the environment to ensure that the behaviors no longer received positive rewards seemed like a plausible solution. Even though our human side seeks immediate and total modification, Jean and Myra learned that moving in smaller steps proved more beneficial to them and the department in the long run and less drastic to others in the short run. But they realized this process takes time. Modification should be a process that involves a coalition of people at various administrative levels and also includes the legal and Human Resources departments (Gunsalus, 2006). Jean and Myra realized that despite their efforts to rectify dysfunction in their department, it would

EPILOG

take a village, not a pair of new faculty members, to modify their departmental culture.

Higher education is conservative, promotes conformity and the status quo, and supports silos and refuges in the name of research. All are seen as normative and often necessary to succeed in research and publication. Jean and Myra noted this behavior in their departmental culture. They realized that in order to succeed at a research institution, they needed to find more quiet time to research and write. While they needed their senior colleagues to show them the way, the reality of researching tended to isolate Myra and Jean from their colleagues, especially the ones who no longer valued research and writing. The conundrum perplexed them further and affected the department's level of collegiality.

Furco and Moely (2012) suggested using voluntary learning community approaches to enhance collegiality, cooperation, learning, collaborative work, and peer networking. These communities can be formal or informal creative safe places, feedback-generating, learning-enhanced, cost-effective opportunities for professional development. What Myra and Jean did not realize is that they created and sustained something parallel to the approach Furco and Moely suggested but isolated themselves in the process. Faculty must be encouraged to practice collegiality by being collaborative and working with others through mentoring and peer relationships doing teaching, research, writing, and service. This participation furthers normative standards for sustained collegial behavioral expectations (Lenze, 1999).

Jean and Myra entered academe before important resources for faculty and administration became readily available. With extensive websites provided by the American Association of University Professors and Inside Higher Education and respected peer-reviewed, research-based articles in scholarly journals, new faculty, tenured faculty, mid-career faculty, bullied faculty, faculty-turned-administrator, and future faculty have assistance at their fingertips. Hopefully, the vignettes in this book used to illustrate faculty life moving along their career path in academe offered each reader insight and direction and perhaps comfort that he or she is not alone. Provided with helpful information, faculty members *can* be successful in academe.

Jean and Myra succeeded in spite of the paucity of professional development and mentoring afforded them early in their careers. Subsequently, each received tenure and made full professor but went onto other institutions as their careers unfolded. In her second position Jean discovered that her university paid far greater attention to professional development for newly hired faculty than her first institution. She took advantage of what they had to offer despite her rank. Myra and Jean continued to research and present. In fact, during their separate careers, they published numerous articles, book chapters, and books and contributed to professional service in addition to teaching and supervising doctoral students. Both Myra and Jean realized the need to mentor graduate students and entry level faculty in order to make their journey in academe a little less bumpy than the road they experienced together years before.

Jean's and Myra's careers, like the vignettes in this book, illustrate a series of highs and lows, up and downs, spikes and plateaus common to all faculty throughout their academic lives. In her ASHE presidential address, Hagedorn (2012) pondered the meaning of academic life. She regarded academic life as a vocation and said, "If we do not find meaning in the life of the mind, in assisting protégés and students to find the pathway to vocation, our vocation deteriorates into a mere job; and happiness and purpose in life likely falter" (p. 487). In order to accomplish this end, faculty may need to alter the silent moments with some constructive input (Bedeian, 2002) that can assist current faculty and benefit future members of the professoriate. Our legacy should be to leave a better collegial culture to the next generation of scholars (Hagedorn, 2012) than we ourselves experienced. We can find success, purpose, and happiness in academe and, then, guide others. Faculty especially needs to work collegially with one another and in concert with administrators to accomplish these outcomes. Hopefully, the best practices and resources provided in this text guide faculty and illuminate their career paths toward greater success.

References

Allen, I.E., & Seaman, J. (2011). *Going the distance: Online education in the U.S., 2011.* Wellesley, MA: Babson Survey Research Group and Quahug Research Group.

Austin, A., & Rice, E. (1998). Making tenure viable: Listening to early career faculty. *American Behavioral Scientist, 41*, 736–754.

Baez, B. (2000). Race-related services and faculty of color: Conceptualizing critical agency in academe. *Higher Education, 39*, 363–391.

Baldwin, R., & Chronister, J. (2001). *Teaching without tenure: Policies and practices for a new era.* Baltimore, MA: Johns Hopkins University Press.

Baldwin, R., DeZure, D., Shaw, A., & Moretto, K. (2008). Mapping the terrain of mid-career faculty at a research university: Implications for faculty and academic leaders. *Change, 4*(5), 46–55.

Barr, R., & Tagg, J. (1995). A new paradigm for undergraduate education. *Change, 27*(6), 13–25.

Barrow, R., & Keeney, P. (Eds.) (2006). *Academic ethics.* Burlington, VT: Ashgate.

Beamish, T. (2000). Accumulating trouble: Complex organization, a culture of silence, and a secret spill. *Social Problems, 47*, 473–498.

Bedeian, A. (2002). The dean's desire: How the darker side of power manifests itself in the office of dean. *Academy of Management Learning and Education, 1*, 164–174.

Belter, R., & duPre, A. (2009). A strategy to reduce plagiarism in an undergraduate course. *Teaching of Psychology, 36*, 257–261.

Bennett, J. (1998). *Collegial professionalism: The academy, individualism, and the common good.* Phoenix, AZ: Oryx Press.

Bennett, J. (2000). Hospitality and collegial community: An essay. *Innovative Higher Education, 25*, 85–96.

Bennett, R. (2005). Factors associated with student plagiarism in a post-1992 university. *Assessment and Evaluation in Higher Education, 30*, 137–162.

REFERENCES

Berberet, J. (1999). The professoriate and institutional citizenship: Toward a scholarship of service. *Liberal Education, 85*(4), 32–39.

Bergquist, W., & Pawlak, K. (2008). *Engaging the six cultures of the academy*. San Francisco, SF: Jossey-Bass.

Beyers, C. (2008). The hermeneutics of student evaluations. *College Teaching, 56*, 102–106.

Bjorkland, W., & Rehling, D. (2010). Student perceptions of classroom incivility. *College Teaching, 58*, 15–18.

Blaszczynski, C., Scott, J., & Green, D. (2009). Refereed publications of vital business educators. *Delta Pi Epsilon Journal, 51*(1), 15–30.

Boice, R. (1996). Classroom incivilities. *Research in Higher Education, 37*, 453–486.

Bolman, L., & Gallos, J. (2011). *Reframing academic leadership*. San Francisco, SF: Jossey-Bass.

Borders, D., Young, L.S., Wester, K., Murray, C., Villalba, J., Lewis, T., et al. (2011). Mentoring promotion/tenure seeking faculty: Principles of good practice within a counselor education program. *Counselor Education and Supervision, 50*, 171–188.

Boyer, E. (1990). *Scholarship reconsidered: Priorities of the professoriate*. Princeton, NJ: Carnegie Foundation for the Advancement of Teaching.

Bray, N. (2008). Proscriptive norms for academic deans—Comparing faculty expectations across institutions and disciplinary boundaries. *Journal of Higher Education, 79*, 692–721.

Bray, N. (2010). The deanship and its faculty interpreters: Do Mertonian norms of science translate into norms for administrators? *Journal of Higher Education, 81*, 284–316.

Bray, N., & Del Favero, M. (2004). Sociological explanations for faculty and student classroom incivilities. In J. Braxton and A. Bayer (Eds.), *Addressing faculty and student classroom improprieties* (pp. 9–19). New Directions in Teaching and Learning #99. Hoboken, NJ: John Wiley and Sons.

Bray, N., & Major, C. (2012). Status of journals in the field of higher education. *Journal of Higher Education, 82*, 479–503.

Britton, D. (2010). Engendering the university through policy and practice: Barriers to promotion to full professor for women in the science, engineering, and math disciplines. In B. Riegraf, B. Aulenbacher, E. Kirsch-Auwarten, and U. Muller (Eds.), *Gender change in academia* (pp. 15–26). Weisbaden, Germany: VS Verlag.

Buch, K., Huet, Y., Rorrer, A., & Roberson, L. (2011). Removing the barriers to full professor: A mentoring program for associate professors. *Change, 43*(6), 38–45.

Buckholdt, G., & Miller, G. (Eds.) (2009). *Faculty stress*. New York, NY: Routledge.

Burgan, M. (2003). Tenure and its discontents. *Academe, 89*, 96.

Burgan, M. (2006). *What ever happened to the faculty? Drift and decision in higher education*. Baltimore, MA: Johns Hopkins University Press.

Burke, L., & James, K. (2010). What factors influence peer ratings of faculty research performance in the Unites States? *Higher Education Management and Policy, 22*, 103–120.

REFERENCES

Cahn, S. (1994). *Saints and scamps: Ethics in academia*. Lanham, MD: Rowman & Littlefield.

Campbell, J. (2000). *Dry rot in the ivory tower*. Lanham, MD: University Press of America.

Carroll, J., & Wolverton, M. (2004). Who becomes a chair? In W. Gmelch and J. Schuh (Eds.), *The life cycle of a department chair* (pp. 3–10). New Directions for Higher Education #126. San Francisco, SF: Jossey-Bass.

Christensen, C., & Eyring, H. (2011). *The innovative university*. San Francisco, SF: Jossey-Bass.

Cipriano, R. (2011). *Facilitating a collegial department in higher education: Strategies for success*. San Francisco, SF: Jossey-Bass.

Clark, B. (1987). *The academic life: Small worlds, different worlds*. Princeton, NJ: Carnegie Foundation for the Advancement of Teaching.

Clawson, D. (2009). Tenure and the future of the university. *Science, 324*, 1147–1148.

Cohen, J. (2004). Failed searches . . . From romance to search committee scholarship. *Journalism and Mass Communication Educator, 59*, 207–210.

Cook, R., Ley, K., Crawford, C., & Warner, A. (2009). Motivators and inhibitors for university faculty in distance and e-learning. *British Journal of Educational Technology, 40*, 149–163.

Cramer, S. (2006). Learning the ropes: How department chairs can help new faculty develop productive scholarship habits. *Reflective Practice, 7*, 525–539.

Creamer, E. (2006). Policies that part: Early career experiences of co-working academic couples. In S. Bracken, J. Allen, & D. Dean (Eds.), *The balancing act* (pp. 73–90). Sterling, VA: Stylus Publishing.

Crumbly, D., Flinn, R., & Reichelt, K. (2010). What is ethical about grade inflation and coursework deflation? *Journal of Academic Ethics, 8*, 187–197.

Curry, B. (2000). *Women in power*. New York, NY: Teacher's College, Columbia University.

Damrosch, D. (1995). *We scholars*. Cambridge, MA: Harvard University Press.

Davis, O.L., Jr. (2001). A view of authentic mentorship. *Journal of Curriculum and Supervision, 17*(1), 1–4.

De George, R. (2003). Ethics, academic freedom, and academic tenure. *Journal of Academic Ethics, 1*(1), 11–25.

Del Favero, M. (2006). An examination of the relationship between academic discipline and cognitive complexity in academic deans' administrative behavior. *Research in Higher Education, 47*, 281–315.

Demb, A., & Wade, A. (2012). Reality check: Faculty involvement in outreach and engagement. *Journal of Higher Education, 83*, 337–366.

Diamond, R. (2002). *Promotion, tenure, and faculty review committees* (2nd ed.). Bolton, MA: Anker Publishing.

Douglas, M. (1986). *How institutions think*. Syracuse, NY: Syracuse University Press.

REFERENCES

Dzeich, B.W., & Weiner, L. (1990). *The lecherous professor* (2nd ed.). Urbana, IL: University of Illinois Press.

Eddy, P., & Gaston-Gayles, J. (2008). New faculty on the block: Issues of stress and support. *Journal of Human Behavior in the Social Environment, 17*(1/2), 89–106.

Eiszler, C. (2002). College students' evaluations of teaching and grade inflation. *Research in Higher Education, 43*, 482–501.

Euben, D. (2002). Publish or perish: The ever-higher publication hurdle for tenure. *Academe, 88*, 78.

Ferdig, R., & Dawson, K. (2006). Faculty navigating institutional waters: Suggestions for bottom-up design on online programs. *TechTrends: Linking Research and Practice to Improve Learning, 50*(4), 28–34.

Field, M., Barg, F., & Stallings, V. (2011). Life after promotion: Self-reported professional development needs and career satisfaction of associate professors. *Journal of Pediatrics, 158*, 175–177.

Filetti, J. (2009). Assessing service in faculty reviews: Mentoring faculty and developing transparency. *Mentoring and Tutoring: Partnerships in Learning, 17*, 343–352.

Fisanick, C. (2006). Evaluating the absent presence: The professor's body at tenure and promotion time. *Review of Education, Pedagogy, and Cultural Studies, 28*, 325–338.

Foote, K. (2009). Toward better mentoring for early career faculty: Results of a study of U.S. geographers. *International Journal of Academic Development, 14*(1), 47–58.

Franke, A. (2001). Making defensible tenure decisions. *Academe, 88*, 32–36.

Furco, A., & Moely, B. (2012). Using learning communities to build faculty support for pedagogical innovations: A multi-campus study. *Journal of Higher Education, 83*, 128–153.

Gallos, J. (2002). The dean's squeeze: Myths and realities of academic leadership in the middle. *Academy of Management Learning and Education, 1*, 174–184.

Geisler, C., Kaminski, D., & Berkeley, R. (2007). The 13th Club: An index of understanding, documenting, and resisting patterns of non-promotion to full professor. *NWSA Journal, 19*, 145–162.

Gibson, S. (2006). Beyond a culture of silence: Inclusive education and the liberation of voice. *Disability and Society, 21*, 315–329.

Gilreath, C., Foster, C., Reynolds, L., & Tucker, S. (2009). Lessons learned by a standing search committee: Developing better practices. *Journal of Academic Librarianship, 35*, 367–372.

Gmelch, W. (2004). The department chair's balancing acts. In W. Gmelch and J. Schuh (Eds.), *The life cycle of a department chair* (pp. 69–84). New Directions for Higher Education #126. San Francisco, SF: Jossey-Bass.

Gouldner, A. (1958). Cosmopolitans and locals: Toward an analysis of latent social roles II. *Administrative Science Quarterly, 2*, 444–480.

REFERENCES

Gravios, J. (2006, December 16). Tracking the invisible faculty. *Chronicle of Higher Education,* 53(7), A8–A9.

Greenberger, E., Lessard, J., Chen, C., & Farruggia, S. (2008). Self-entitled college students: Contributions of personality, parenting, and motivational factors. *Journal of Youth and Adolescence, 37,* 1193–1204.

Gunsalus, C.K. (2006). *The college administrator's survival guide.* Cambridge, MA: Harvard University Press.

Hagedorn, L.S. (2012). The meaning of academic life. *Review of Higher Education, 35,* 485–512.

Hall, D. (2002). *The academic self: An owner's manual.* Columbus, OH: Ohio State University Press.

Hard, S., Conway, J., & Moran, A. (2006). Faculty and college student beliefs about the frequency of student academic misconduct. *Journal of Higher Education, 77,* 1058–1080.

Harris, M., & Hartley, M. (2011). Witch-hunting at Crucible University: The power and peril of competing organizational ideologies. *Journal of Higher Education, 82,* 691–719.

Hauptman, R. (2002). Dishonesty in the academy. *Academe, 88*(6), 39–44.

Hearn, J., & Anderson, M. (2002). Conflict in academic departments: An analysis of disputes over faculty promotion and tenure. *Research in Higher Education, 43,* 503–529.

Hecht, I. (2004). The professional development of department chairs. In W. Gmelch and J. Schuh (Eds.), *The life cycle of a department chair* (pp. 27–44). New Directions for Higher Education #126. San Francisco, SF: Jossey-Bass.

Heggins, W. (2004). Preparing African Americans for the professoriate: Issues and challenges. *Western Journal of Black Studies, 28,* 354–364.

Heike, A., Hazen, H., & Theobold, R. (2010). Classroom incivilities: The challenge of interaction between college students and instructors in the United States. *Journal of Geography in Higher Education, 34,* 439–462.

Herreid, C., & Full, R. (2010). How to survive as academic job interview. *Journal of College Science Teaching, 39*(3), 10–15.

Hirschy, A., & Braxton, J. (2004). Effects of student classroom incivilities on students. In J. Braxton and A. Bayer (Eds.), *Addressing faculty and student classroom improprieties* (pp. 67–76). New Directions in Teaching and Learning #99. Hoboken, NJ: John Wiley and Sons.

Hodge, D., & Lacasse, J. (2011). Ranking disciplinary journals with Google Scholar H-Index: A new tool for constructing cases for tenure and promotion and other professional decisions. *Journal of Social Work Education, 47,* 579–596.

Hora, M. (2012). Organizational factors and instructional decision-making: A cognitive perspective. *Review of Higher Education, 35,* 207–235.

REFERENCES

Howard, R. (2001) *A Beautiful Mind*. US, Imagine Entertainment.

Howze, P. (2008). Search committee effectiveness in determining a finalist pool: A case study. *Journal of Academic Librarianship, 34*, 340–353.

Hurt, J. (2011). Non-tenure track women faculty: Opening the door. *Journal of the Professoriate, 4*(1), 96–124.

Huston, T., Norman, M., & Ambrose, S. (2007). Expanding the discussion of faculty vitality to include productive but disengaged senior faculty. *Journal of Higher Education, 78*, 493–522.

Hutchens, N. (2011). Using a legal lens to better understand and frame issues shaping the employment environment of non-tenure track faculty members. *American Behavioral Science, 55*, 1443–1460.

Jacobs, S. (2006). Denied tenure, Skocpol alleged sexual discrimination. *The Harvard Crimson*, June 5. www.thecrimson.com/article/2006/6/5/denied-tenure-skocpol-alleged-sexual-discrimination (retrieved January 17, 2012).

Jawitz, J. (2007). New academics negotiating community of practice: Learning to swim with the big fish. *Teaching in Higher Education, 12*, 185–197.

Kekes, J. (1996). Academic corruption. *Monist, 79*, 564–576.

Kezar, A. (2012). Bottom-up/top-down leadership: Contradictions or hidden phenomenon. *Journal of Higher Education, 83*, 725–766.

Kezar, A., & Sam, C. (2010). Understanding the new majority of non-tenured faculty in higher education. *ASHE Higher Education Report, 36*(4), 19–47.

Kezar, A., & Sam, C. (2011). Understanding non-tenure track faculty: New assumptions and theories for conceptualizing behavior. *American Behavioral Science, 55*, 1419–1442.

Knight, W. (2010). Sink or swim: Navigating the perilous waters of promotion and tenure—What's diversity got to do with it? *Studies in Art Education: A Journal of Issues and Research in Art Education, 52*(1), 84–87.

Koblinsky, S., Kuvalanka, K., & McClintock-Comeaux, M. (2006). Preparing future faculty and family professionals. *Family Relations, 55*(1), 29–43.

Lampman, C., Phelps, A., Bancroft, S., & Beneke, M. (2009). Contrapower harassment in academe: A survey of faculty experience with student incivility, bullying, and sexual attention. *Sex Roles, 60*, 331–346.

Landrum, R.E., & Clump, M. (2004). Department search committees and the evaluation of faculty applicants. *Teaching of Psychology, 31*, 12–17.

Lang, J. (2005). *Life on the tenure track*. Baltimore, MA: Johns Hopkins University Press.

Lenze, L. (1999). Accountability for faculty welfare. In R. Menges and associates, *Faculty in New Jobs* (pp. 310–327). San Francisco, SF: Jossey-Bass.

Lessor, R. (2008). Adjudicating frame shifts and frame disputes in the new millennial university: The role of the dean. *American Sociologist, 39*(2/3), 114–129.

REFERENCES

Levin, J., & Shaker, G. (2011). The hybrid and dualistic identity of full time non-tenure track faculty. *American Behavioral Science, 55*, 1461–1484.

Levy, E., & Rakovski, C. (2006). Academic dishonesty: A zero tolerance professor and student registration choices. *Research in Higher Education, 47*, 735–754.

Lippman, S., Bulanda, R., & Wagenaar, T. (2009). Student entitlement. *College Teaching, 57*, 197–204.

Llorens, J. (2010, November). A culture of silence threatens to impede a safer workplace. *Training and Development, 64*(11), 22.

Mabrouk, P. (2007). Promotion from associate to full professor. *Analytical and Bioanalytical Chemistry, 388*, 987–991.

MacFarlane, B. (2011). Professors as intellectual leaders: Formation, identity, and role. *Studies in Higher Education, 36*(1), 57–73.

McDowell, J., Singell, L., & Ziliak, J. (2011). Gender and promotion in the economics profession. *Industrial and Labor Relations, 54*, 224–244.

Meyerson, D. (2003). *Tempered radicals: How everyday leaders inspire change at work*. Boston: Harvard Business School Press.

Miller, S., Brueggeman, Blue, B., & Shephard, D. (1997). Present perfect and future imperfect: Results of a national survey of graduate students in rhetoric and composition programs. *College Composition and Communication, 48*, 392–409.

Minton, C., Fernando, D., & Ray, D. (2008). Ten years of peer-reviewed articles in counselor education: Where, what, who? *Counselor Education and Supervision, 48*, 133–143.

Mitchell, R. (2009). Online education and organizational change. *Community College Review, 37*(1), 81–101.

Namie, G., & Namie, R. (2000). *The bully at work*. Naperville, IL: Sourcebooks.

Nathan, R. (2005). *My freshman year*. Ithaca, NY: Cornell University Press.

Orlans, H. (2002). Collegiality or congeniality? *Change, 34*(2), 8–9.

Ornstein, M., Stewart, P., & Drakich, J. (2007). Promotion at Canadian universities: The intersection of gender, discipline, and institution. *Canadian Journal of Higher Education, 37*(3), 1–25.

Orr, R., Williams, M., & Pennington, K. (2009). Institutional efforts to support faculty in online teaching. *Innovative Higher Education, 34*, 257–268.

Palmer, P. (1998). *The courage to teach*. San Francisco. SF: Jossey-Bass.

Pan, D., Tan, G., Ragupathi, K., Booluck, K., Roop, R., & Ip, Y. (2009). Profiling teacher and teaching using descriptors derived from qualitative feedback: Formative and summative applications. *Research in Higher Education, 50*, 73–100.

Plater, W. (1998). Using tenure: Citizenship within the new academic workforce. *American Behavioral Scientist, 41*, 680–715.

Pololi, L. (2005). Mentoring faculty in academic medicine. *Journal of General Internal Medicine, 20*, 866–870.

REFERENCES

Poskanzer, S. (2002). *Higher education law: The faculty*. Baltimore, MA: Johns Hopkins University Press.

Reybold, L. E. (2008). The social and political structuring of faculty ethnicity in education. *Innovations in Higher Education, 32*, 279–295.

Rice, M., & Miller, M. (2001). Faculty involvement in planning for the use and integration of instructional and administrative technology. *Journal of Research in Computing in Education, 33*, 328–336.

Roach, V., & El-Khawas, E. (2010). Gender equity in the university: The unmet agenda. *Forum on Public Policy: A Journal of the Oxford Round Table, 2*, 1–18.

Romeu, J. (2002/2003). Course administrations: The often neglected component of technology infusion. *Journal of Educational Technology Systems, 31*(1), 35–43.

Ross, E. (1910). *Social control*. New York, NY: Macmillan.

Schlesinger, A. (n.d.). *BrainyQuote.com*. www.brainyquote.com/quotes/quotes/a/arthurmsc109503.html (retrieved July 24, 2012).

Schneckenberg, D. (2009). Understanding the real barriers to technology-enhanced innovation in higher education. *Educational Research, 51*, 411–424.

Senge, P. (1990). *The fifth discipline*. New York, NY: Doubleday.

Shils, E. (1997). *The academic ethic and other essays in higher education*. Chicago, IL: University of Chicago Press.

Silverman, F. (2004). *Collegiality and service for tenure and beyond*. Westport, CT: Praeger.

Simplicio, J. (2007). A closer look at the truth behind the hiring process: How colleges really hire. *Education, 128*, 256–261.

Slaughter, S. (2001). Professional values and the allure of the market. *Academe, 87*(5), 22–26.

Slevin, J. (1993). Finding voices in the culture of silence. *Liberal Education, 79*(2), 4–10.

Slevin, J. (2000). Preserving critical faculties. *Liberal Education, 86*(3), 20–27.

Snyder, M. (2000). State of the profession: Tenure in perspective. *Academe, 86*, 103.

Sorcinelli, M.D. (2002). New conceptions of scholarship for a new generation of faculty members. In K. Zahorski (Ed.), *Scholarship in the postmodern era: New venues, new values, new visions* (pp. 41–48). New Directions for Teaching and Learning #90. Hoboken, NJ: Wiley and Sons.

Stanley, C., & Algert, N. (2007). An exploratory study of the conflicting management styles of department heads in a research university setting. *Innovative Higher Education, 32*, 49–65.

Stark-Wroblewski, K., Ahlering, R., & Brill, F. (2007). Toward a more comprehensive approach to evolutionary teaching effectiveness: Supplementing student evaluations of teaching with pre-post learning measures. *Assessment and Evaluation in Higher Education, 32*, 403–415.

Stimpson, C. (2000). A dean looks at tenure. *Academe, 88*, 34–37.

REFERENCES

Tauer, L., Fried, H., & Fry. W. (2007). Measuring efficiencies of academic departments within a college. *Education Economics, 15*, 473–489.

Thomas, E., & Gillespie, D. (2008). Weaving together undergraduate research, mentoring of junior faculty, and assessment: An interdisciplinary program. *Innovative Higher Education, 33*, 29–38.

Thomas, J., & Schuh, J. (2004). Socializing new chairs. In W. Gmelch and J. Schuh (Eds.), *The life cycle of a department chair* (pp. 11–25). New Directions for Higher Education #126. San Francisco, SF: Jossey-Bass.

Thompson, C. (2006). Unintended lessons: Plagiarism and the university. *Teachers College Record, 108*, 2439–2449.

Tillman, L. (2011). Mentoring African American faculty in predominantly white institutions. *Research in Higher Education, 42*, 295–325.

Tozer, A. W. (2007). *Mystery of the Holy Spirit*. Alachura, FL: Bridges Logos Foundation.

Twale, D., & De Luca, B. (2008). *Faculty incivility: The rise of the academic bully culture and what to do about it*. San Francisco, SF: Jossey-Bass.

Twale, D., & Shannon, D. (1996). Gender differences among faculty in campus governance: Nature of involvement, satisfaction, and power. *Initiatives, 57*(4), 11–19.

Valle, M., & Schultz, K. (2011). The etiology of top-tier publications in management: A status attainment perspective on academic career success. *Career Development International, 16*, 220–237.

Waltman, J., Bergom, I., Hollenshead, C., Miller, J., & August, L. (2012). Factors contributing to job satisfaction and dissatisfaction among non-tenure track faculty. *Journal of Higher Education, 83*, 411–434.

Washburn, J. (2005). *University, Inc.: The corporate corruption of higher education*. New York, NY: Basic Books.

Weick, K. (1976). Educational organizations as loosely coupled systems. *Administrative Science Quarterly, 21*, 1–19.

Weidman, J., Twale, D., & Stein, E. (2001). *Socialization of graduate and professional students in higher education: A perilous passage?* ASHE –ERIC Monograph 28(3). San Francisco, SF: Jossey-Bass.

Weiser, I. (2012). Peer review in the tenure and promotion process. *College Composition and Communication, 63*, 645–654.

Westerman, J., Bergman, J., Bergman, S., & Daly, J. (2012). Are universities creating millennial narcissistic employers? An empirical examination of narcissism in business students and its implications. *Journal of Management Education, 36*(1), 5–32.

Wickersham, L., & McElhany, J. (2010). Bridging the divide: Reconciling administrative and faculty concerns regarding online education. *Quarterly Review of Distance Education, 11*(1), 1–12.

Worthen, K. (2004). Discipline: An academic dean's perspective on dealing with plagiarism. *Brigham Young University Education and Law Journal, 2004*(2), 441–448.

REFERENCES

York, A., & Vance, J. (2009). Taking library instruction into the online classroom: Best practices for embedded librarians. *Journal of Library Administration, 49*, 197–209.

Youn, T., & Price, T. (2009). Learning from the experiences of others: The evolution of faculty tenure and promotion rules in comprehensive institutions. *Journal of Higher Education, 80*, 204–237.

Zellers, D., Howard, V., & Barcic, M. (2008). Faculty mentoring programs: Re-envisioning rather than reinventing the wheel. *Review of Educational Research, 78*, 552–588.

Index

AAUP *see* American Association of University Professors
academic culture 1–8
academic honesty code violation 29–31
Academic Leader 99, 107
The Academic Self 55
acceptance of publication 78–9
acclimation 41, 52–5, 58–9
acting in tandem 96–7
administrative support 40–41
administrator perspectives 91–6; female deans 94–5; hot-headedness 95–6; taking advantage of new post 91–3; yearly performance appraisal 93–4
ambiguity 69–71, 74
American Association of Higher Education 99
American Association of University Professors 55, 75, 93–4, 99–100, 107, 115, 118
American Council on Education (AAUP) 99
Anderson, M. 71
andragogy 30
angst 47; *see also* fear
annual performance appraisal 93–4
ASHE *see* Association for Study of Higher Education
assistant professorship 10–11
Association of American Colleges and Universities 100

Association for Study of Higher Education 23, 119
asynchronous delivery 45, 47
August, L. 105
Austin, A. 70, 72
autonomy 4, 7, 29, 72, 80

Baez, B. 88
balance of power 53–4
Bancroft, S. 34
Barg, F. 113–14
Barr, R. 44
barriers to social change 89
Becoming an Academic Writer 82
Becoming a Successful Early Career Researcher 75
Bedeian, A. 96
Belter, R. 36
Benek, M. 34
Bennett, John 3–4, 6, 56
Berberet, J. 88
Bergom, I. 105
Bergquist, W. 4
Berkeley, R. 114
best practice 37, 46–7, 55, 73–5, 80–81, 89–90, 98–9, 106–7, 114–15, 220–23
Best Practices for Teaching with Emerging Technologies 47
Bjorklund, W. 33
Blanchard, Kenneth 56

131

INDEX

Blasycyznski, C. 80
Blue, D. 59
Boice, Robert 34, 36, 75
Bolman, Lee 56
Booluck, K. 32
Boyer, E. 76
Braxton, John 36, 55
Bray, N. 36, 97
Brueggeman, B. 59
Buch, K. 114
bullying 51, 53–4, 118
Burke, L. 81
business contracts 64–6

Cabell's Directory of Publishing 61, 82
Cahn, S. 5
Campbell, J. 4–5
campus character 48–9
campus service 83–90; best practices 89–90; debriefing 88–9; introduction 83–8; resources 90
Carnegie Classification 67–8
challenging policy 86–7
character of departments 48–9
cheating 36–7
Christensen, E. 44
Clark, Burton 6
classroom teaching 24–38; best practices 37; debriefing 31–7; introduction 24–31; resources 38
coasting 60, 113
cognitive mapping 99
Cohen, J. 21
collegial culture 3–5
collegiality 1–8, 57–69, 73–4, 86–9, 94, 118; collegial culture 3–5; faculty role obligations 2–3; paradoxes and ironies 6–8
committee search chair 10–11
complacency 17, 28, 31, 54, 67–8, 94
conference networking 76
conferencing 76–82; best practices 81–2; debriefing 80–81; introduction 76–80; resources 82

confidentiality 25–6, 35, 85
conservatism 4–5, 118
constructive criticism 99
consumerism 31–2
contrapower harassment 34
Cook, R. 46
corporatization of higher education 100–104; unresolved conflict 101–4
"courting the candidate" 21
Cramer, S. 98
Crawford, C. 46
credibility 96, 113
Crumbly, D. 35
culture of privacy 112
culture of silence 21, 35, 63, 75, 117

de facto tenure 68–70
De George, R. 7
debriefing: campus service/institutional citizenship 88–9; classroom teaching/evaluation 31–7; conferencing/publishing 80–81; departmental culture 52–4; faculty/administrative relationships 96–8; off the tenure track 104–6; pathways to full professor 112–14; road to tenure 69–73; search committee process 17–22; teaching online 44–6
Del Favero, M. 36, 99
delivering virtual education 39–44; administrative support 40–41; fraud 42–4; technical support 41–2
DeLuca, B. 55, 107
Demb, A. 89
departmental culture 48–56; best practices 55; debriefing 52–4; introduction 48–9; resources 55–6; vulgarity and insensitivity 49–52
departmental protocol 17, 27–9
departmental welcome 51–2
The Department Chair Primer 56
Diamond, Robert 75

INDEX

disengagement 100
disrespect 28
disruption 24, 27, 30, 33–6, 44, 105
disruptive innovation 44
Douglas, M. 6
Drakich, J. 112
Drucker, Peter 56
duPre, A. 36
dysfunction 18–19, 48–9, 54–5, 75, 117–18

e-learning strategies 45; *see also* teaching online
early tenure and promotion bids 62–4
Educause 47
Eiszler, C. 32
El-Khawas, E. 112
enculturation 55
entitlement 27, 34–5
ethics 2–3, 16–18, 21–2
Euben, D. 69
evaluation 24–38
expecting the unexpected 48–56
Eyring, H. 44

Faculty Incivility 55
faculty research collaboration 4, 46, 58, 70, 76, 80, 83, 118
faculty role obligations 2–3
faculty search committees 9–23; best practices 22–3; debriefing search committee process 17–22; introduction 9–17; resources 23
Faculty Stress 56
faculty teaching, student evaluation of 25–6
faculty–administrator relationships 91–9; best practices 98–9; debriefing 96–8; introduction 91–6; resources 99
fear 45, 47, 70
female deans 94–5
Field, M. 113–14

Filetti, J. 19
finding correct match 9–23
first and second chances to full 108–111
Fisanick, C. 32
Flinn, R. 35
fraud 42–4
full professorship, pathways to 108–115
Furco, A. 118

Geisler, C. 114
gender tide shift 11
generation of presentations 76–80; acceptance and rejection 78–9; invisible conference colleagues 79–80; manipulating the system 77–8
getting with the program 87–8
Getting Tenure at a University 75
Gmelch, W. 98
good fit 21, 72
Good Practice in Tenure Evaluation 99
Goodson, Patricia 82
graduate council members 84–5
graduate faculty status 61–2
Gravios, J. 100
Green, D. 80
grievances 30–31, 34–7, 83, 102–7
guidelines manual 23
Gunsalus, C.K. 105
gypsy scholars 100

Hagedorn, L.S. 119
Hall, Donald 55
harassment 7, 34–5, 96, 101, 103, 106
Harvard 44
Hazen, H. 34
hazing new faculty members 50–51
Hearn, J. 71
Heike, A. 34
heterocosm, academe as 4
hierarchy 48

133

INDEX

Hirschey, A. 36
Hollenshead, C. 105
honesty codes 29–31, 35
hot-headedness 95–6
how to teach college students 24–31; faculty protocol 27–9; semester length 26–7; student evaluation 25–6; violation of academic honesty codes 29–31
Howze, P. 18
Huet, Y. 114
Hurt, J. 100
hybrid courses 42, 47

incivility 3, 33–5, 55, 100–102
inclusion 18, 26, 77, 79
Inside Higher Education 23, 115, 118
institutional citizenship 83–90
integrity crisis 7, 43
intellectual reciprocity 3
inter-rater reliability 81
internal department chair search 13–15
invisible conference colleagues 79–80
Ip, Y. 32
ironies within collegium 6–8
issue resolution 116–19

James, K. 81
Jawitz, J. 53
Journal of Faculty Development 38

Kaminski, D. 114
Kamla, Barbara 82
Kezar, A. 97, 100

Lampman, C. 34
Lang, James 6, 18, 32, 72, 75, 88
last chance to promotion 111–12
Leaming, Deryl 56
Lessor, R. 96
leveraging search 12–13
Levin, J. 106

Ley, K. 46
"life of the mind" 2–3
Life on the Tenure Track 75
Llorens, J. 117

McElhany, J. 44
MacFarlane, B. 97
manipulating the system 77–8
marketing for the cash cow 5
Marsh, Herbert W. 38
maturity of performance 21
mediation 102–3, 105
mentoring 2–7, 23, 46, 52–5, 58–9, 63–8, 73, 78–82, 116–19
Meyerson, D. 97
Miller, J. 105
Miller, M. 46
Miller, S. 59
mission 96–7, 105
Moely, B. 1118
motivation 32, 46, 71, 88, 112–13
Moxley, Joseph 75
My Freshman Year 28

Nash, John 1
Nathan, Rebekah 28
National Center for Educational Statistics 107
natural selection 80
Nobel Prize 1
non-tenure track 100–107; best practices 106–7; debriefing 104–6; introduction 100–104; resources 107

obligations of faculty 2–3
off the tenure track *see* non-tenure track
Ohio State University 56
on the tenure track 57–75
on-the-job training 91
online teaching 39–47
open communication 117
optimism 25, 98

134

INDEX

Orlans, H. 3
Ornstein, M. 112

P&T *see* promotion and tenure
Pacansky-Brock, Michelle 47
Palmer, P. 6
Pan, D. 32
pandering 35
paradoxes within collegium 6–8
paternalism 63–4, 69
pathways to full professorship 108–115; best practices 114–15; debriefing 112–14; introduction 108–112; resources 115
patriarchy 48
Pawlak, K. 4
peer evaluation 102–3
perceived power 6–7
perpetuating status quo 6–7, 18
personal gain 12–13
Phelps, A. 34
plagiarism detection 29–30, 36–8
Plagiarism, the Internet, and Student Learning 38
Plater, W. 72
political allegiance 45, 49
Poskaner, S. 21
power broking 99
power misalignment 49
Practical Guide to University and College Management 99
pre-tenure review 59–60, 73
prejudice 17–18
Preparing for Promotion, Tenure, and Annual Review 75
Price, T. 69
Principles of Good Practice 99
professoriate 1–8
Professors Behaving Badly 55
Professors as Writers 75
promotion and tenure 57–69; business contracts 64–6; de factor tenure 68–9; early tenure and promotion bids 62–4; graduate faculty status 61–2; pre-tenure review 59–60; "up or out tenure situation" 66–8
promotion and tenure committee 85–6
promotion to full 108–112; first and second chances 108–111; last chance 111–12
psychic energy 88
Publish, Don't Perish 75
publishing 76–82

Ragupathi, K. 32
Reframing Academic Leadership 56
Rehling, D. 33
Reichelt, K. 35
rejection of publication 78–9
research expectation 72–3
retaliation 31, 36, 87, 102, 106
rewards for service 84, 88, 91–3
Reybold, L. E. 7
Rice, E. 70, 72
Rice, M. 46
Roach, V. 112
road to tenure 57–75
roadblocks 59
Roberson, L. 114
Romeu, J. 45–6
Roop, R. 32
Rorrer, A. 114

Safe Assignment 38
sanctions 35–6
Schlesinger, Arthur 44
Scholarship Reconsidered 76
Schuh, J. 99
Schultz, K. 80
Scott, J. 80
screening 20
searching for truth 2–3, 58
self-advocacy 117
self-aggrandization 5
self-esteem 34
semester length 26–7
sensitivity 49–52

135

INDEX

service function roles 83–8; challenging policy 86–7; getting with the program 87–8; graduate council's members 84–5; promotion and tenure committee 85–6
serving on search committee 9–17; committee search chair 10–11; experienced hire 16–17; external department internal candidate 15–16; internal department chair search 13–15; leveraging search 12–13
serving time-in-rank 108–112; first and second chances to full 108–111; last chance 111–12
sexual harassment 101–2; *see also* harassment
Shaker, G. 106
Shannon, D. 88
Shepherd, D. 59
Shils, Edward 2–3, 7
"shoot, aim, ready" 39–47
Silverman, F. 58, 74, 98–9
Slaughter, S. 33
socialization 21–2, 34, 48, 55, 73, 91, 96, 98
Sorcinelli, M.D. 72, 99
Stallings, V. 113–14
Stewart, P. 112
stress 1–3, 36, 56, 95–8, 103
student evaluation of faculty teaching 25–6
sustaining discipline 2–3
Sutherland-Smith, Wendy 38
symbolic integration 6
synchronous delivery 45, 47

Tagg, J. 44
taking advantage of new post 91–3
Tan, G. 32
teaching online 39–47; best practices 46–7; debriefing 44–6; introduction 39–44; resources 47
technical support 41–2

tenure track 57–75; best practices 73–5; debriefing 69–73; introduction 57–69; resources 75
Tenure on Trial 75
Theda Skocpol case 58
Theobold, R. 34
Thomas, J. 99, 999
Thomson, Pat 82
Thomson Reuters Web of Knowledge 82
threatening behavior 34, 37
time-in-rank service 108–112
tolerance 18
Tools for Dossier Success 75, 115
Tozer, A. W. ix
Trinity College 56
Turnitin 38
Twale, Darla 55, 88, 107

University of South Carolina 56
unresolved conflict 101–4
untenured faculty members 19, 22
"up or out tenure situation" 58, 66–8
upholding ethical standards 2–3

Valle, M. 80
Vance, J. 47
vetting 20
victimization 54
violation of honesty codes 29–31
vulgarity 18, 49–52; departmental welcome 51–2; hazing of new members 50–51
vulnerability 54–5, 66, 100–102, 105, 107

Wade, A. 89
Wagner, Neal 75
Waltman, J. 105
Warner, A. 46
Washburn, J. 4
Weick, K. 44–5
Wickersham, L. 44
women's advancement 114
Working with Problem Faculty 56

Worthen, K. 36
Writing for Peer Reviewed Journals 82
Writing Your Way to Success 75

yelling 34
York, A. 47
Youn, T. 69

Taylor & Francis
eBooks
FOR LIBRARIES

ORDER YOUR FREE 30 DAY INSTITUTIONAL TRIAL TODAY!

Over 23,000 eBook titles in the Humanities, Social Sciences, STM and Law from some of the world's leading imprints.

Choose from a range of subject packages or create your own!

Benefits for you
- ▶ Free MARC records
- ▶ COUNTER-compliant usage statistics
- ▶ Flexible purchase and pricing options

Benefits for your user
- ▶ Off-site, anytime access via Athens or referring URL
- ▶ Print or copy pages or chapters
- ▶ Full content search
- ▶ Bookmark, highlight and annotate text
- ▶ Access to thousands of pages of quality research at the click of a button

For more information, pricing enquiries or to order a free trial, contact your local online sales team.

UK and Rest of World: **online.sales@tandf.co.uk**
US, Canada and Latin America: **e-reference@taylorandfrancis.com**

www.ebooksubscriptions.com

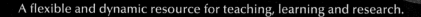
A flexible and dynamic resource for teaching, learning and research.